THEN NOW

ABINGDON

OPPOSITE: Depicted in this *c.* 1950 postcard is Abingdon's Barter Theatre, the State Theatre of Virginia. Founded in 1933 during the Depression by Robert Porterfield to provide his fellow actors a livelihood bartering entertainment for goods and produce from the local population, this world-famous theatre has produced many of show business's "greats."

THEN NOW

ABINGDON

Donna Gayle Akers

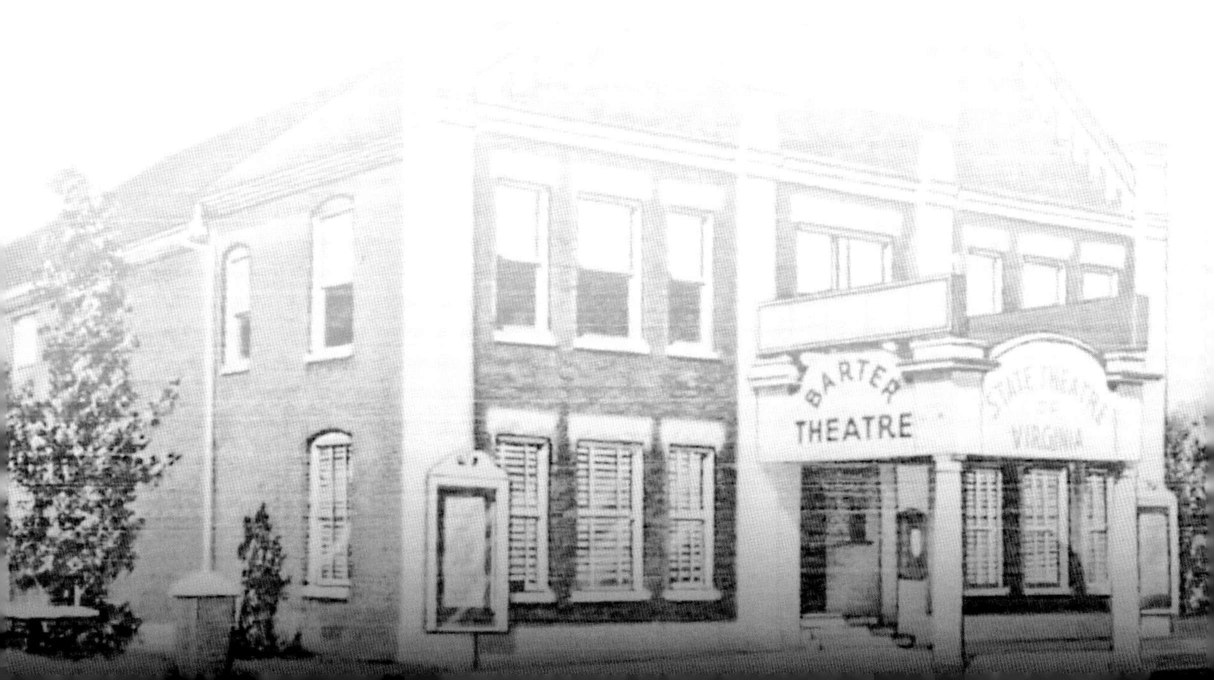

ISBN 978-0-7385-8658-8

Library of Congress Control Number: 2010926293

Published by Arcadia Publishing
Charleston, South Carolina

Printed in the United States of America

For all general information, please contact Arcadia Publishing:
Telephone 843-853-2070
Fax 843-853-0044
E-mail sales@arcadiapublishing.com
For customer service and orders:
Toll-Free 1-888-313-2665

Visit us on the Internet at www.arcadiapublishing.com

On the Front Cover: The date of June 3, 1908, was significant to residents, as a grand ceremony took place for the dedication of a symbol of courage, the Confederate Soldier memorial. Over 500 people dressed in their Sunday best attended the gala, while Elizabeth Stuart, grandniece of Gen. J.E.B. Stuart, unveiled the statue. The statue was intended to mourn the Civil War—the sons lost and the hardships endured, including two Union raids through the town. The stately courthouse is the fifth building for the county government, built in 1869 after the fourth courthouse was burned by Union soldiers. As vehicle traffic increased, the statue was moved from the middle of Main Street to a safer location in the side yard of the courthouse. (Historical Society of Washington County.)

On the Back Cover: Shown in this image of the first Burley Tobacco Festival Parade in 1948 on Main Street near Wall Street is the Vance Supply Co. wagon, escorted by Elmer Rosenbaum. Held annually in September, this community agricultural celebration is now known as the Washington County Fair, since few farmers now grow Burley tobacco, long a staple regional crop. (Courtesy Elmer Rosenbaum.)

Contents

For Jennifer L. DeHart (1966–2010)
My best friend forever, who taught me how to truly live by battling ovarian cancer for over five years, although it finally took her too soon on May 11, 2010, age 44 years. She believed in me more than anyone.

And for Owen and Riley
Blood of my blood, ninth-generation descendants of Washington County pioneers, who inspire, amaze, and will likely make history of their own.

And to all those pioneers and ancestors who settled in this fertile valley and carved home from wilderness.

Acknowledgments

This compilation of images from Abingdon's history provides a window into history and shows changes from a frontier fort to a thriving community. Not intended to be a formal and thorough history, this volume attempts to merely document some of the historical changes through historic and modern photographs. Much of the information for the captions was gathered from documented histories, printed sources, and personal stories. The author's best efforts were made to verify major events and facts, but conflicting data and sketchy information made fact-finding challenging.

An endeavor of any type is never accomplished alone. The completion of this book would not have been possible without the prior research by local historians, the preservation of photographs by individuals, Douglas Patterson (longtime Abingdon photographer), the Town of Abingdon, and the Historical Society of Washington County, Virginia, and the generosity of all of the above in allowing me to use their information, interview them, and scan their images of Abingdon's history. I would like to thank the following individuals who provided images, historic information, and contacts for this volume: the Town of Abingdon, Lorena Harris Bolling, Jimmie Lou Bowden, Lowry Bowman, Lynda Campbell, Dot Cowan, Janice Taylor Duncan, Allen Gregory, Margaret Harris, Edith Maiden Hatcher, the Historical Society of Washington County, Garrett Jackson, Stephen Jett, Irene Meade Johnson, Peggy Johnson, Charles G. Jones, Nancy King, Verna Lowe Mahaffey, Myra Worsham Martin, Norma Counts Meade, Jane Oakes, Douglas Patterson, Elmer Rosenbaum, Sean Taylor, Fred Tweed, Michael Worrell, and Emmitt Yeary.

The assistance of Elizabeth Bray, my editor with Arcadia Publishing, was integral to completing this book in terms of technical assistance and moral support. As always, thanks to my two sons, Owen and Riley, and my family in Abingdon for their support and love.

Unless otherwise noted, all "now" images are from the author's collection.

INTRODUCTION

As Abingdon and Washington County change with the times, this book provides an invitation for Abingdonians and Washington County residents to remember the earlier days—the businesses, streets, public buildings, churches, schools, and houses and homes. Visitors, transplanted folks to the area, and residents will observe the town's efforts, mostly successful, to preserve its historic built environment. Abingdon has experienced many changes, from an outpost on the frontier to a thriving commercial center, to a bustling government and trade center exporting by railroad, to the cultural, arts, antique, governmental, and historical locus that it is today.

Abingdon, Virginia, incorporated in 1778, was named in honor of Martha Washington's ancestral parish in England, a fitting name since the surrounding Washington County was named for Pres. George Washington. No community can exist separate from its environment, and accordingly, the settlement, progress, and development of the town and county is molded by these. Lying in the Great Valley region of Virginia, the county is braided by the three branches of the Holston River—the North, Middle, and South Forks—which made fertile soils, provided transportation in the early days, and produced much developable land.

At the time of European exploration from across the eastern mountains, this land was a rich hunting ground for the Cherokees, Shawnees, and various smaller groups. However, abundant Native American archeological remains show the area was occupied for thousands of years before that time. In 1746, Thomas Walker and Loyal Land Company surveyors were the first group to survey the area, opening up this western territory to settlers hungry for new land. Thousands of pioneers from eastern Virginia, the Shenandoah Valley, Maryland, Pennsylvania, and North Carolina began to stream into this "Garden of Eden" beginning in the mid to late 1700s. However, the Native Americans resented the taking of their hunting grounds and were stirred up by the French and Indian War, resulting in bloody conflicts with the settlers between the 1750s and late 1700s. After numerous fatalities and settlers taken captive, pioneers fled up the Valley Road into the settled areas, but they returned in large numbers after the Revolutionary War and the French and Indian War ended. Black's Fort, built by Joseph Black in 1774 near today's Abingdon trailhead of the Virginia Creeper Trail, was a location for the first Washington County court and provided shelter for hundreds of pioneers during Native American attacks.

Washington County was divided from larger Fincastle County in 1776, and later, the counties of Buchanan, Dickenson, Wise, Russell, Scott, Smyth, Lee, and Tazewell were created from Washington County. Although these hardy settlers lived in the hinterlands, they participated in the battles for our nation's freedom when 400-some brave men answered a muster call in 1780 from Gen. William Campbell. These "Over the Mountain Men" mustered with other volunteers at Sycamore Shoals, Tennessee, and marched over the mountains to defeat the British at the Battle of King's Mountain, South Carolina, considered a turning point in the Revolutionary War. By 1782, the town was comprised of a log courthouse, Dunn's Hotel, a log jail, and three taverns. Continued growth made the town the center for postal delivery for southwest Virginia and eastern Kentucky from 1793 to 1835.

Historical records reflect the rapid early growth: by 1835, the town had 150–200 houses, 2 academies, 2 hotels, 3 taverns, 1 flourmill, 9 mercantile houses, 3 groceries, 1 wool and 2 cotton factories, 4 tanyards, 10 blacksmith shops, 1 hat factory and store, 6 wheelwrights and wagon makers, 2 cabinet factories, and 2 boot and shoe manufactories. These businesses reflect the economy and the time period, when many items were hand-made and horses and wagons were the transportation mode. At this time, Abingdon grew to be a major stop on the Great Wagon Road into Kentucky, a place to trade for a new wagon with Hagy Wagon Company, and one of the last places to bank. Another factor contributing to the economic success of the town was that many of the wealthy landowners, such as the Kings and Prestons, gained wealth from salt production in nearby Saltville and invested it in houses, land, and schools here. Salt was critical for food preservation at this time and was a precious commodity. Accordingly, the best road in the region in 1803 was a toll road between Saltville and Abingdon.

In 1856, a line for the Virginia and Tennessee Railroad linked Lynchburg, Virginia, with Abingdon and Bristol, Virginia/Tennessee. The rail lines allowed passengers to travel and goods to be imported and exported. Grocery stores in Abingdon shipped farm produce, animal skins, and other items to cities on the eastern seaboard. In 1900, the Virginia-Carolina completed a rail line to Damascus in order to harvest timber. By 1911, the Norfolk and Western Railway bought out Virginia-Carolina and extended these lines to Elkland, North Carolina. Smaller communities grew up along the smaller depots, such as Damascus, Glade Spring, Meadowview, and Alvarado.

The Civil War hit the area hard, with scarcities of basic goods, many sons lost or wounded, and a dip in economic prosperity. Attempting to destroy the salt mines in nearby Saltville and cut off railroad lines, the Union army conducted two raids within the town, resulting in property losses from fires.

Just 20 years later, according to Chataigne's 1888–1889 *Virginia Gazetteer*, Abingdon was "noted for its fine schools and colleges, bracing and salubrious climate, besides being a place of considerable importance as a manufacturing, commercial and shipping center."

Although a rural region, education has always been a priority. In 1888–1889, a total of 105 white and 21 "colored" schools existed in the county before consolidation took place. However, Abingdon and the surrounding county have also had a number of private schools and colleges as well, including Abingdon Male Academy, Jackson Female Institute, Martha Washington College, Stonewall Jackson Institute, Southwest Virginia Institute for Young Ladies, Virginia Intermont, and Emory and Henry College. The excellent railroad system and location on major roads attracted industrialists and capitalists in the late 1800s and early 1900s. The timber boom lasted almost 25 years and was a key source of employment for the population, although the land was left devastated. Woodworking plants, sawmills, extract plants, and other industries were built near the timber and the rail lines, which were extended into the mountains to harvest the timber. However, as the trees were depleted, the main cargo for the railroads disappeared, so mail and passenger train service was discontinued in 1962. Reflective of the ingenuity in this area, Abingdon, led by Mayor French Moore II, acquired the old Virginia-Carolina railroad right-of-way from Abingdon to Whitetop Mountain and converted it to a recreational trail for pedestrians and bicyclists known as the Virginia Creeper Trail.

During the Depression, Robert Porterfield started the Barter Theatre by allowing the locals to barter food and goods for tickets, which provided his out-of-work acting friends with jobs and food. Many famous thespians started their acting careers at the Barter, and it became the State Theatre of Virginia in 1946. During the 1970s, the downtown area lost many businesses when they closed or moved to the new strip and shopping malls. However, beginning in the 1980s and continuing today, business owners and local government worked to revitalize and redevelop downtown. Today, the downtown is an eclectic mixture of antique stores, cafés, restaurants, retail stores, and offices. Abingdon has always attracted visitors, and tourism remains a significant economic contributor. Few folks visit without planning their next trip because of Abingdon's unique blend of Southern charm, historic buildings, arts, and culture.

CHAPTER

STREET SCENES

TRAVELLED AND SEEN

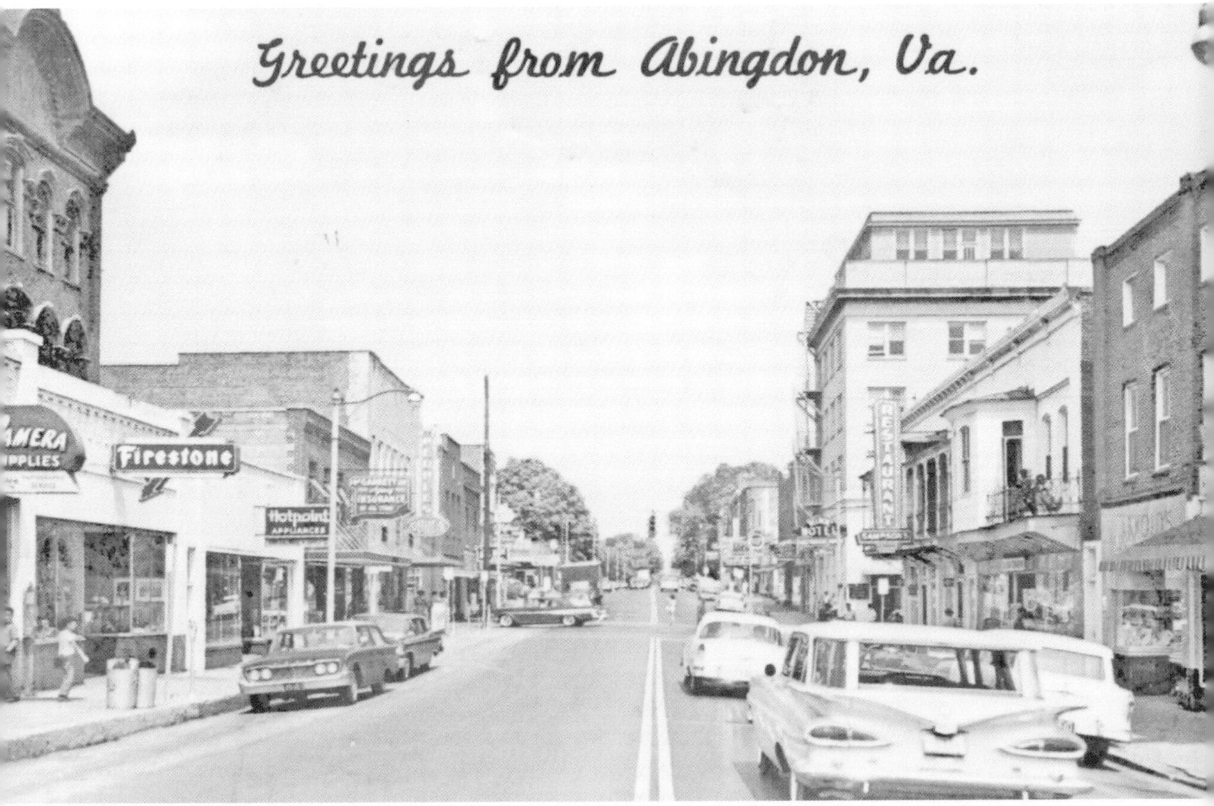

ABINGDON POSTCARD GREETINGS. This postcard shows the town's early promotional efforts, advertising the Barter Theatre, the Martha Washington Inn, and tobacco production and agriculture. Along the left of the photograph can be seen Patterson Photography Studio, Vance Hardware, Garrett Insurance, and People's Drug, while on the right are the Belmont Hotel and restaurant and People's National Bank. (Myra Worsham Martin.)

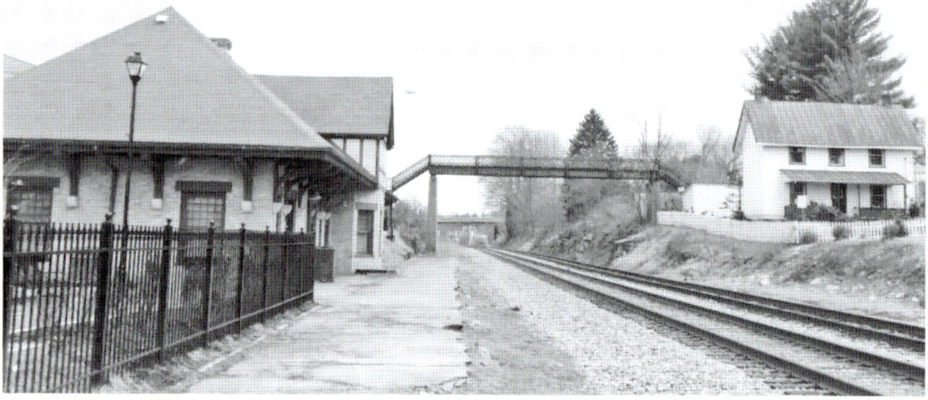

Abingdon Depot. With rail service beginning in 1856, this Abingdon Depot building (1909) started the Abingdon Branch, which terminated in West Jefferson, North Carolina. First owned by the Virginia and Tennessee Railroad, then Norfolk and Western, the tracks connected the town to trade and commercial centers. The tracks are still used by Norfolk Southern Railroad, but the depot has been renovated and now holds the offices of the Historical Society of Washington County, Virginia. (Town of Abingdon.)

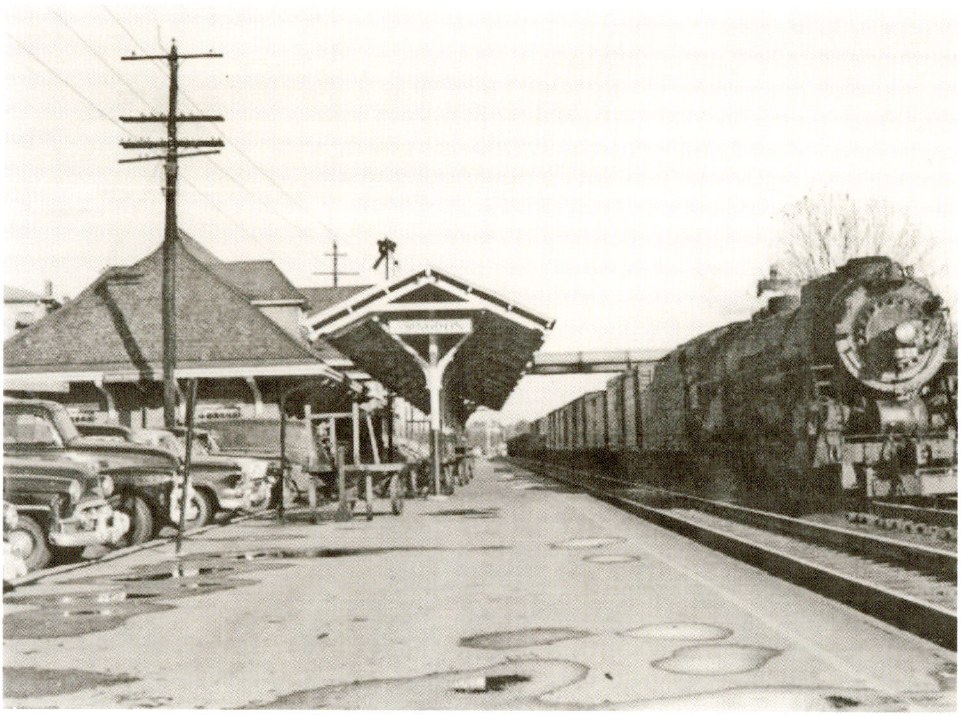

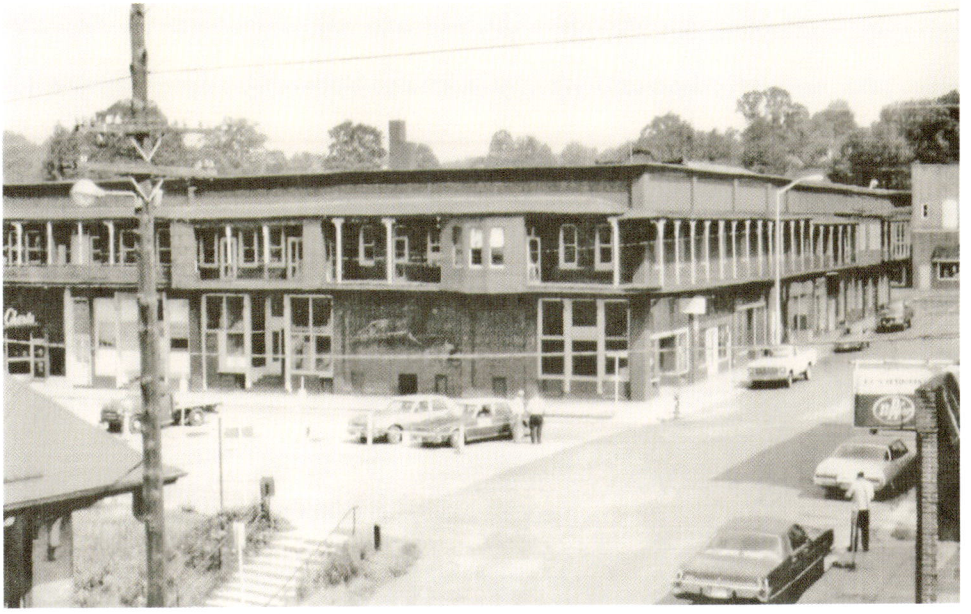

Belmont Hotel. The well-known Belmont Hotel (later the Eureka) was built by Henry Hopkins Scott in 1887 at the corner of Wall and Main Streets. This two-story building contained a restaurant and various commercial shops on the bottom floor, including grocery stores, pool halls, a barbershop, and shoe stores. Parties and dances were held in the 1940s and 1950s in the building. The hotel was torn down before 1981 to construct the present-day post office. (Town of Abingdon.)

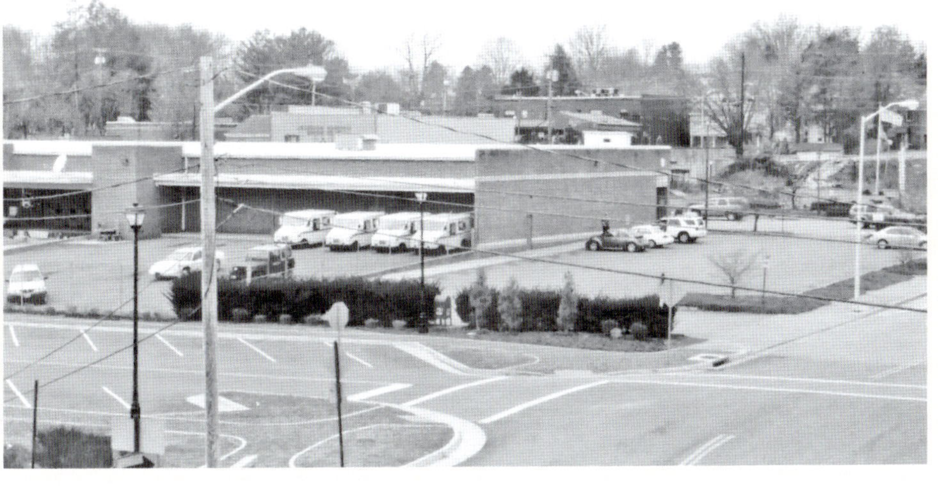

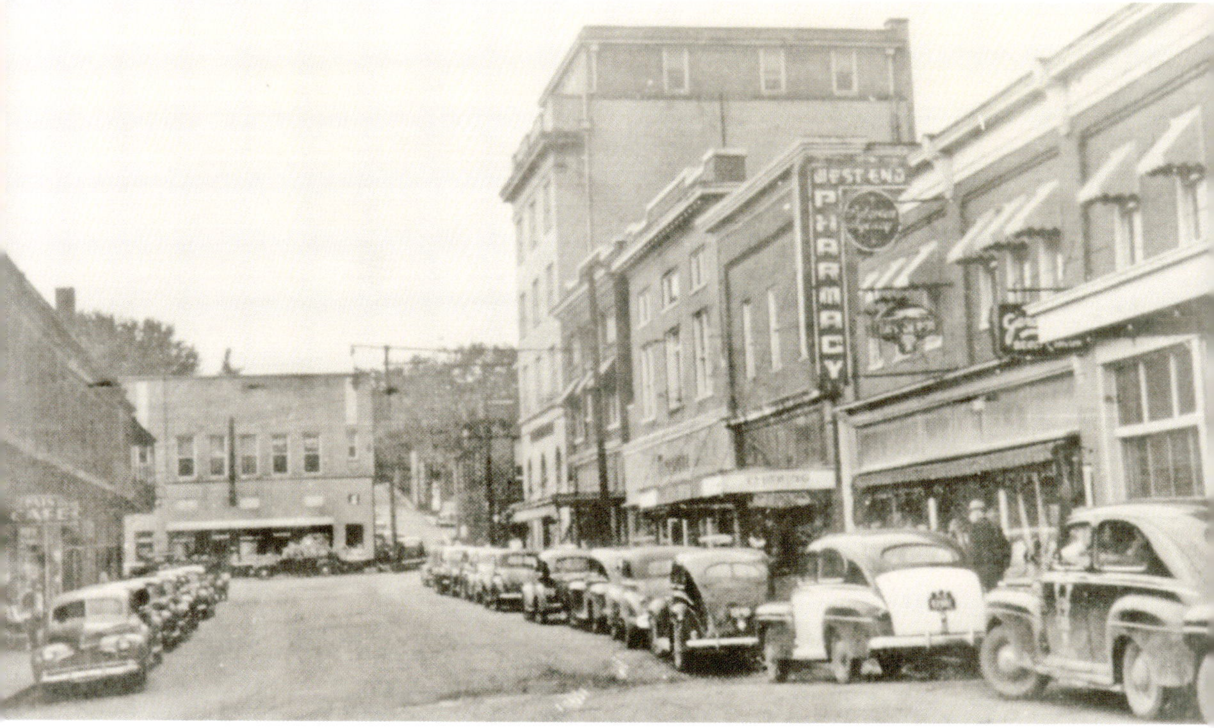

WALL STREET AROUND 1940. Located on busy Wall Street, the popular West End Pharmacy is visible on the right of the above photograph. Founded as Dr. Gold's Drug Store in 1886, it became West End Pharmacy and evolved into Maiden's Drug Store (1916) when purchased by W. A. Maiden, remaining a gathering place. Today, most of these buildings on Wall Street, with the exception of the building in the background at the end of the street, and the bank building, have been demolished. (Edith Maiden Hatcher.)

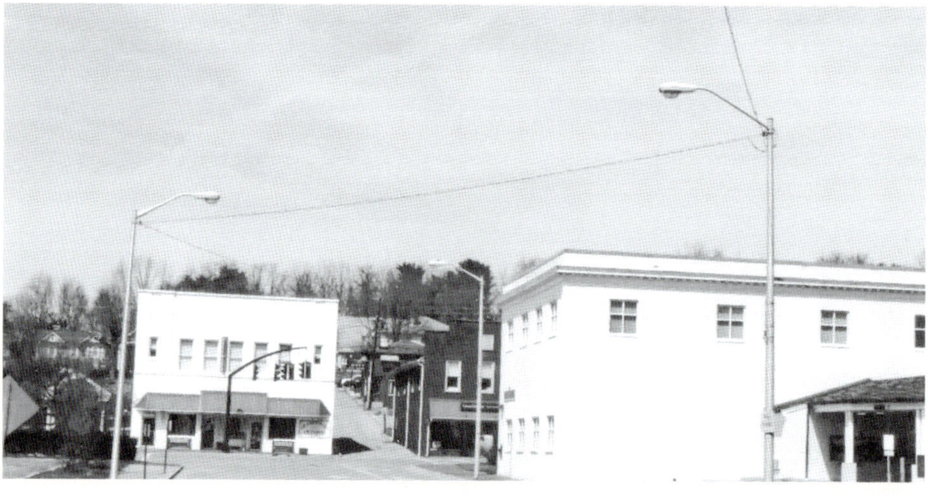

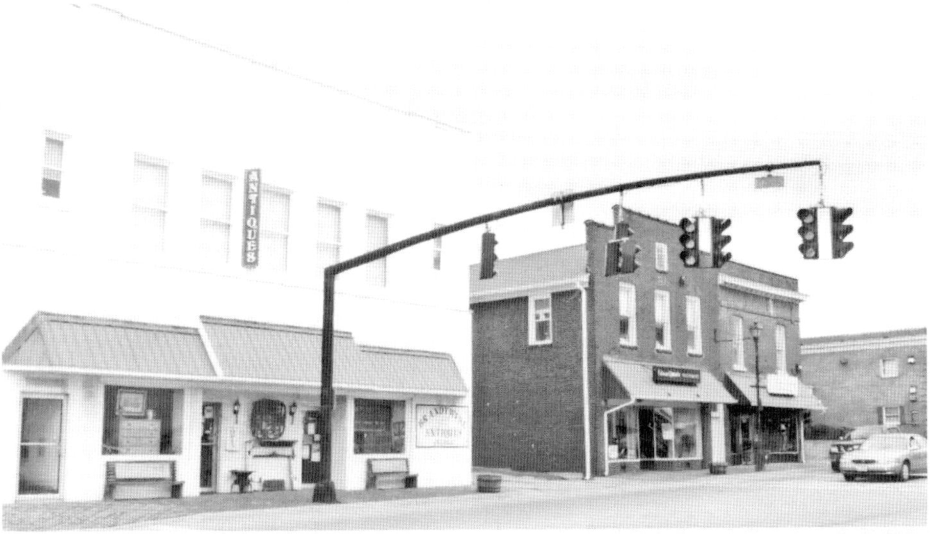

Washington County Tobacco Festival, 1948. The vintage photograph below depicts the first parade for the Burley tobacco festival as it proceeds along West Main Street. Dapper Elmer Rosenbaum walks beside the Vance Supply wagon. From left to right, the businesses are A. W. Crosswhite Men's Store, G. A. Pruner Dry Goods, the Farmer's Exchange Bank, Sam Snead Electrical, and Yellow Cab Company. These buildings are still standing and now house offices and antique stores. (Elmer Rosenbaum.)

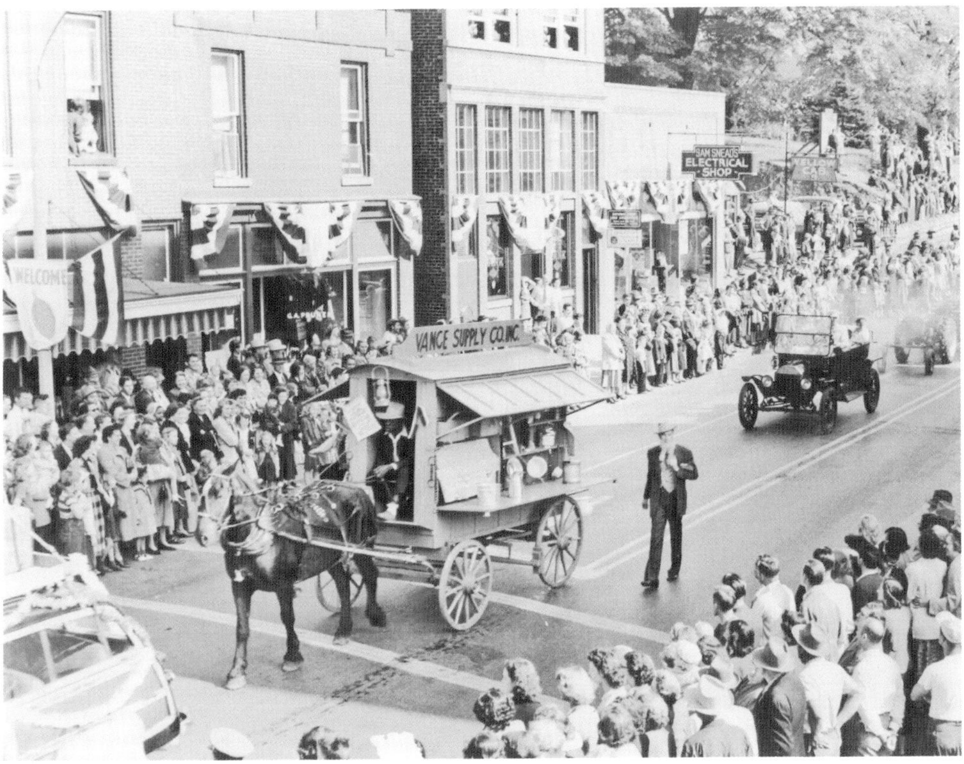

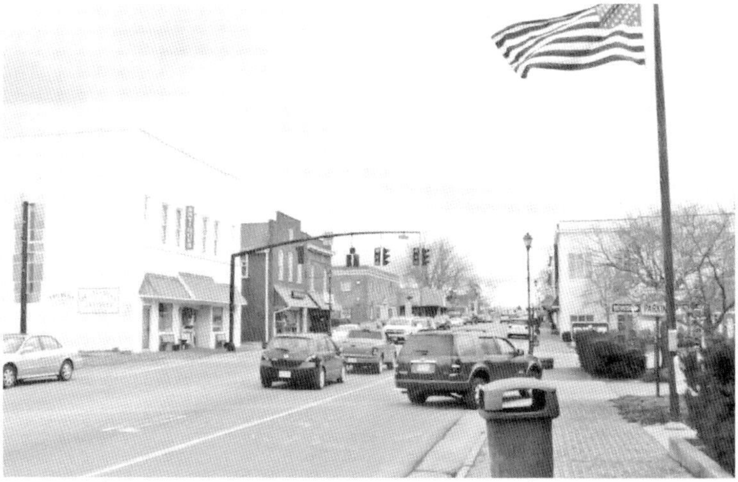

WEST MAIN STREET, 1950. Cars are parked along both sides of West Main Street, where businesses provided clothing, tools, meals, lodging, theater, and recreation. Along the left side of the photograph, the following businesses are visible: a drive-in, Morrell's Shoe Shop, Vance Hardware, and People's Drugstore. Along the right side, businesses include Bundy's, Arnold Jewelry store, the A&P grocery store, Sampson's Café, the Belmont Hotel, and People's Bank. (Town of Abingdon.)

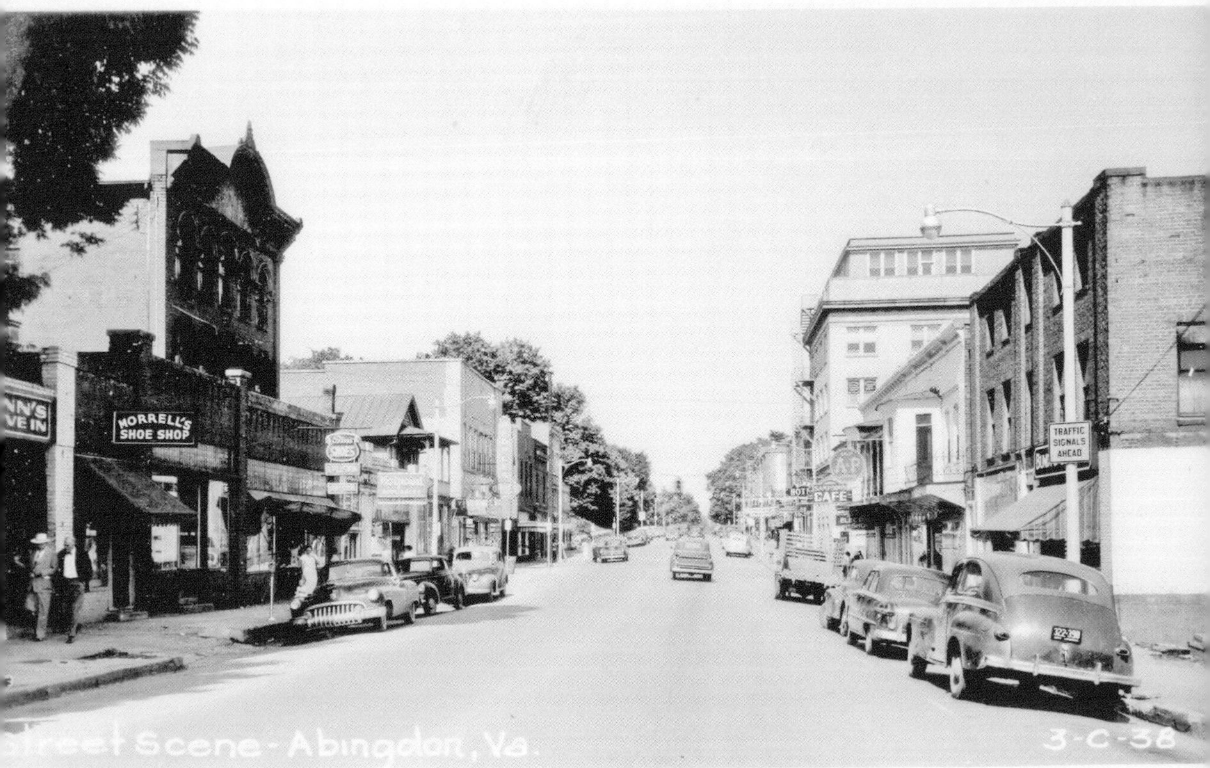

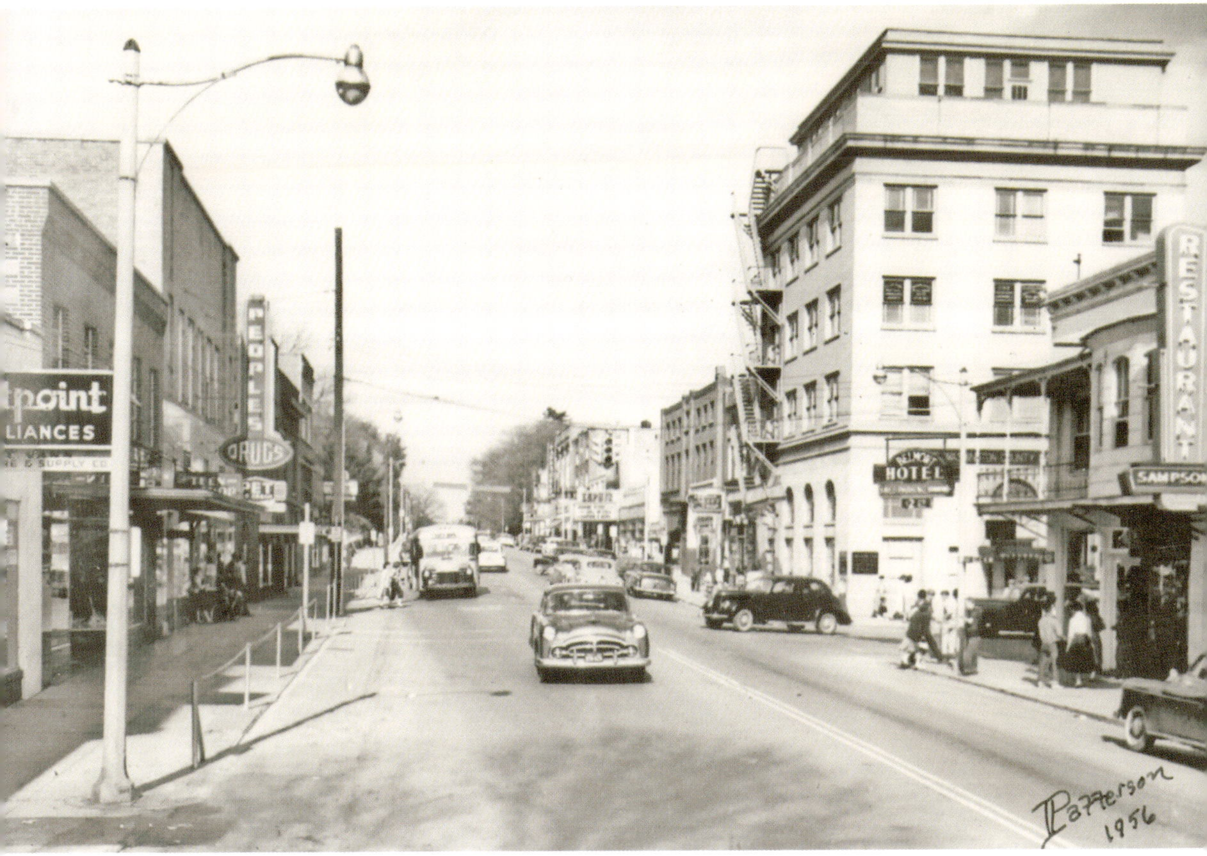

West Main Street. In the 1956 photograph above, taken by local photographer Doug Patterson, a town bus is visible that provided transportation within town limits. On the right, the Belmont Restaurant and Hotel, People's National Bank, the Sweet Shop, and Zephyr Theatre are visible. Vance Hardware, the Teen Shop, and People's Drug Store are visible to the left. Today, some of the buildings remain, but the uses have changed. (Doug Patterson photograph courtesy Allen Gregory.)

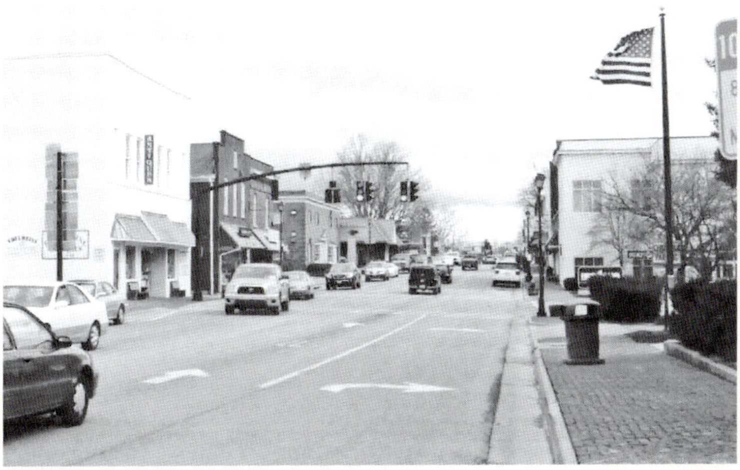

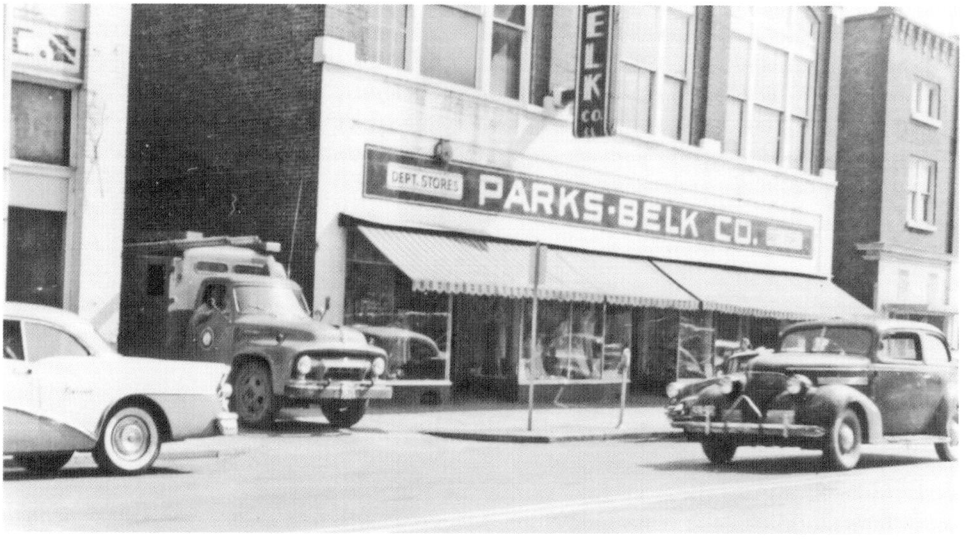

Parks Belk Company. Shown above in the late 1950s, this tall downtown brick building was occupied for many years by Parks Belk Company, a popular department store that was part of the national Belk's chain. A trip to town wasn't complete without shopping at Parks Belk, even if it were merely window shopping. The business was closed by the 1980s, and retail and offices occupy the building today. (Peggy Johnson.)

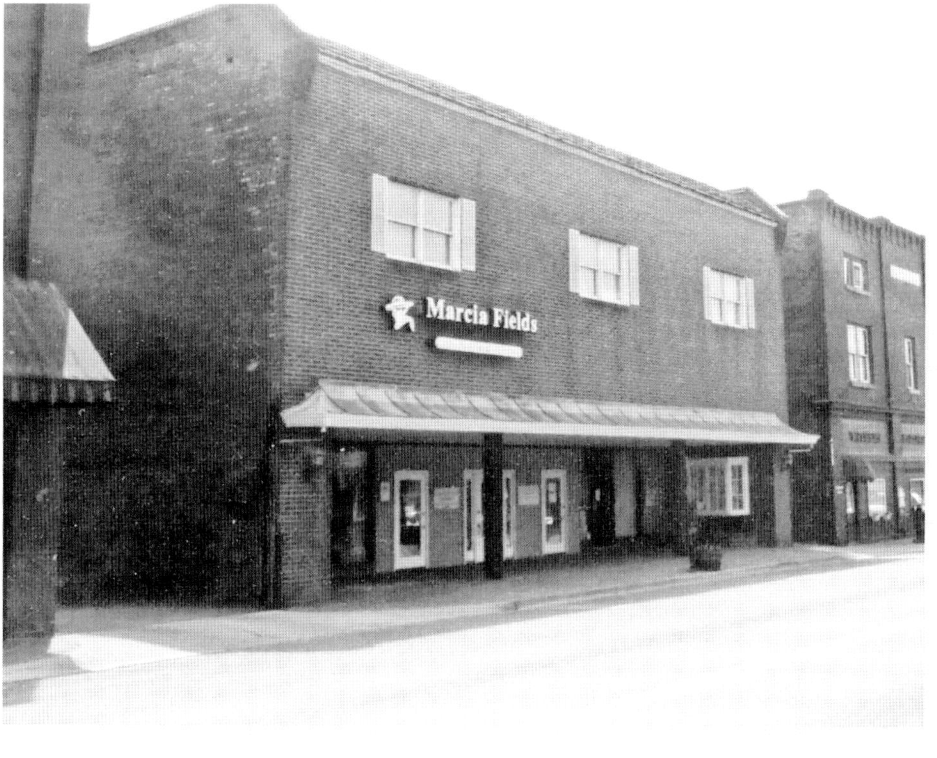

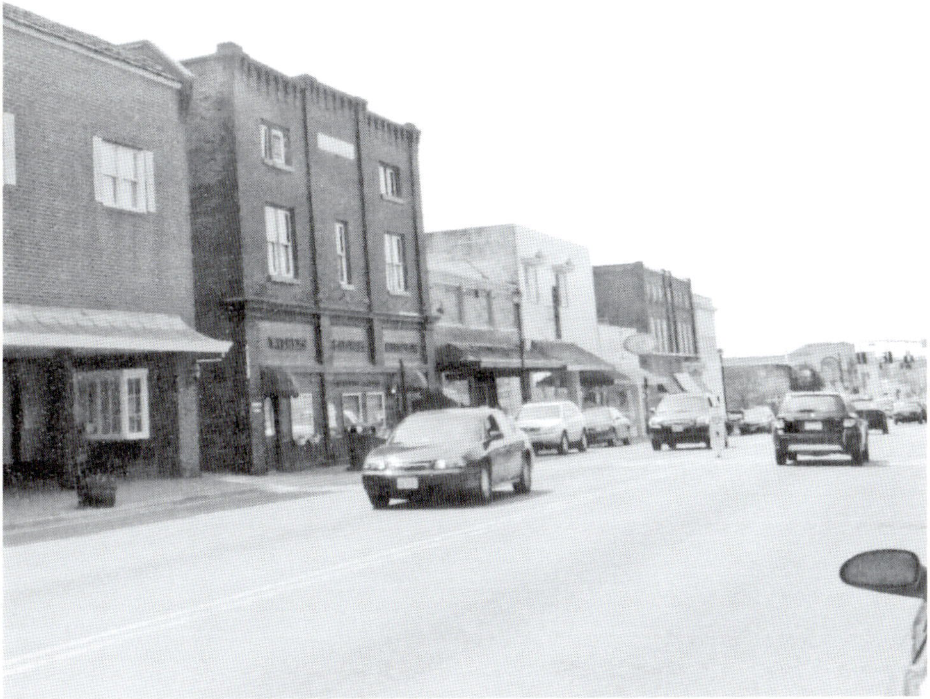

West Main Street in 1966. West Main Street and its then-thriving businesses are shown in the 1966 photograph below. From left to right are Louis Sterchi Furniture (1937), Zephyr Theatre (1939), the Scott Building (1914), and People's National Bank (1923). It is remarkable that these older buildings are still in existence in downtown Abingdon, although the uses have changed through the years. (Peggy Johnson.)

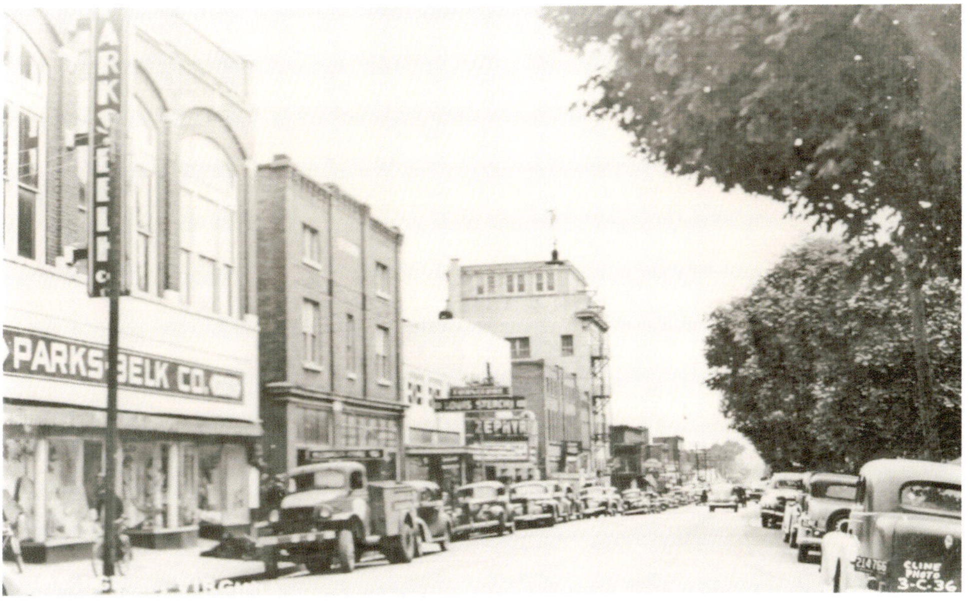

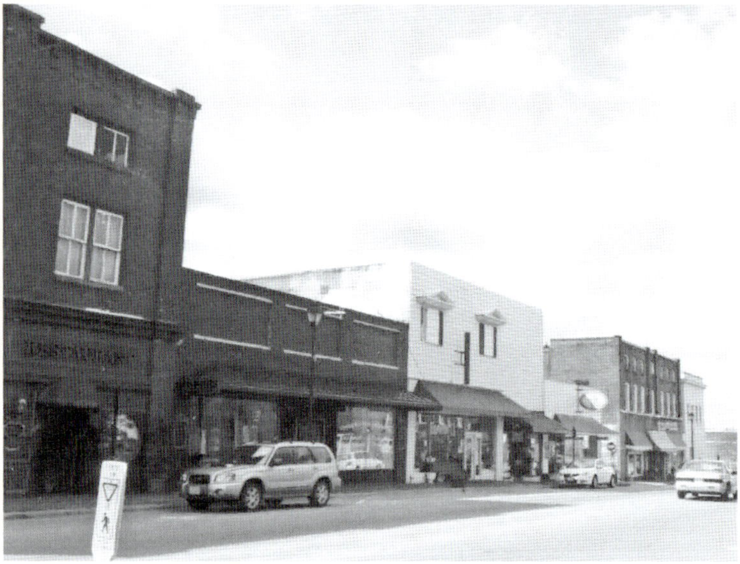

STERCHI FURNITURE AND ZEPHYR THEATRE, 1965. Two major businesses in the downtown West Main Street area are visible in the photograph below. The Zephyr marquee reads "Peter O'Toole in *Lord Jim* also *The Bounty Killer*." Lois Sterchi Furniture, located across from the courthouse since 1918, moved into this 1937 brick building and operated until 1990. The Zephyr Theatre was established in 1939 and operated until around 1963 as the town's first modern movie theater. Today, the buildings house retail businesses. (Peggy Johnson.)

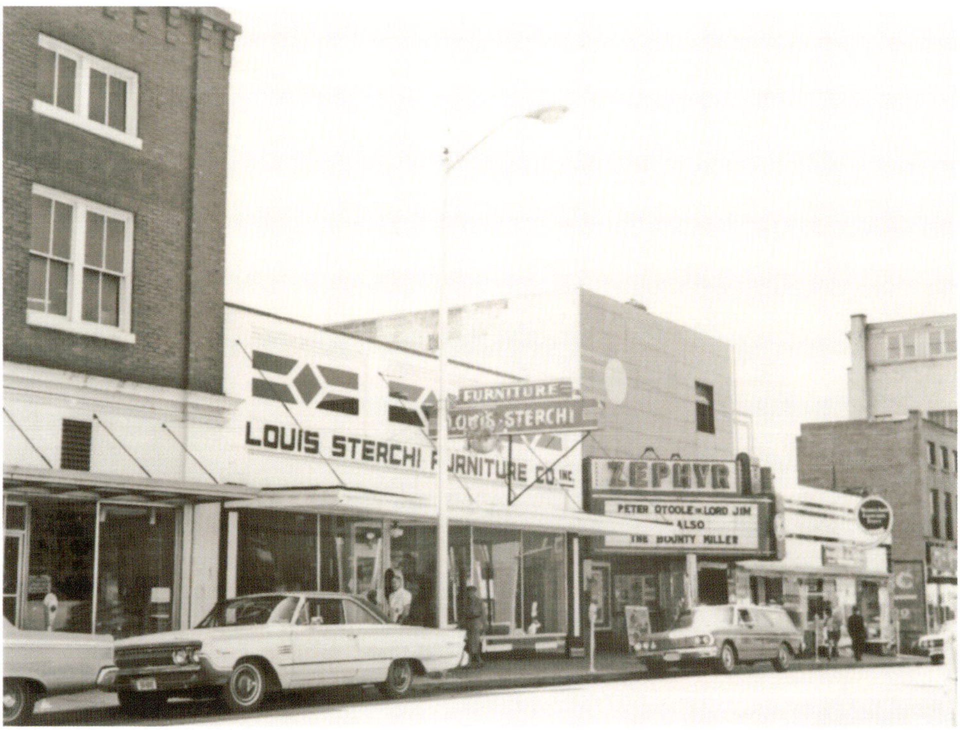

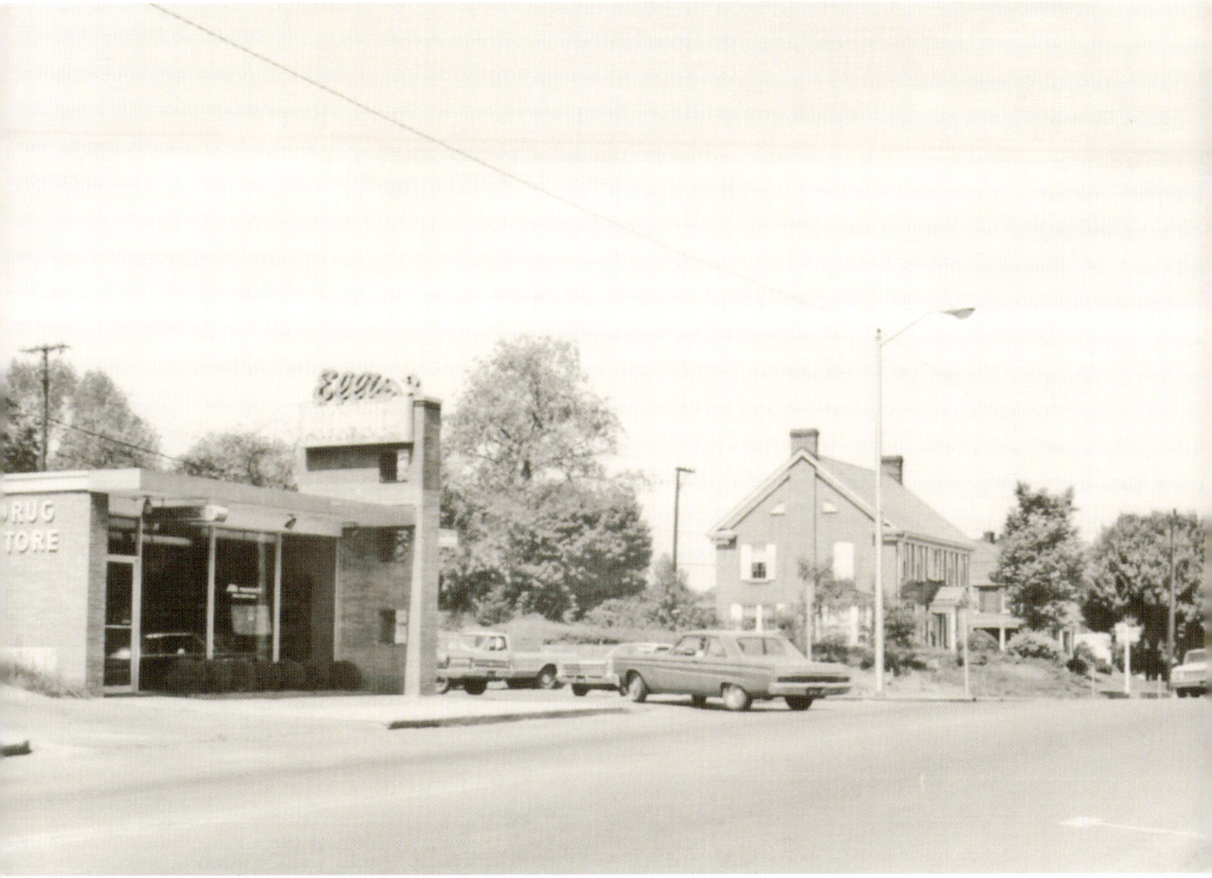

Ellis Drug Store. Ellis Pharmacy first began in the old Farmer's Exchange building before Harold Ellis constructed this building on West Main Street in 1959. The photograph shows the building before the second story was added in the 1970s. The Hurt House, the substantial brick house in the background, was built for Mary Helen Bickley and her husband Wallace Hurt. Today, Ellis Soda Shop occupies the drugstore. (Peggy Johnson.)

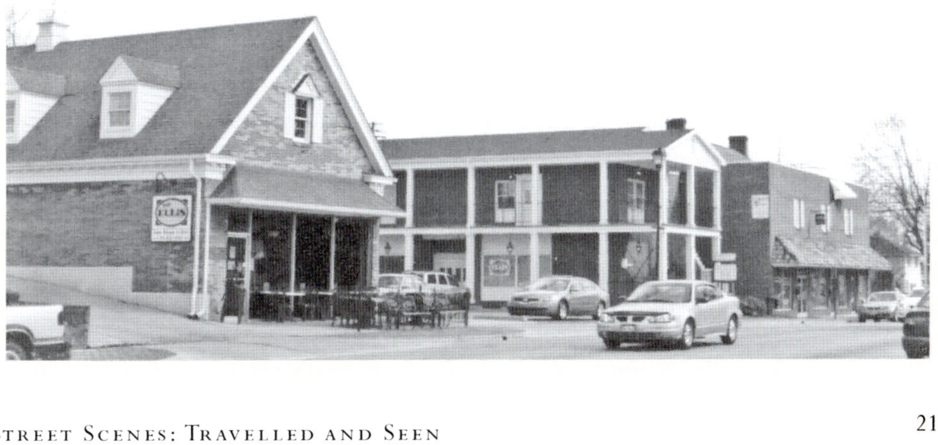

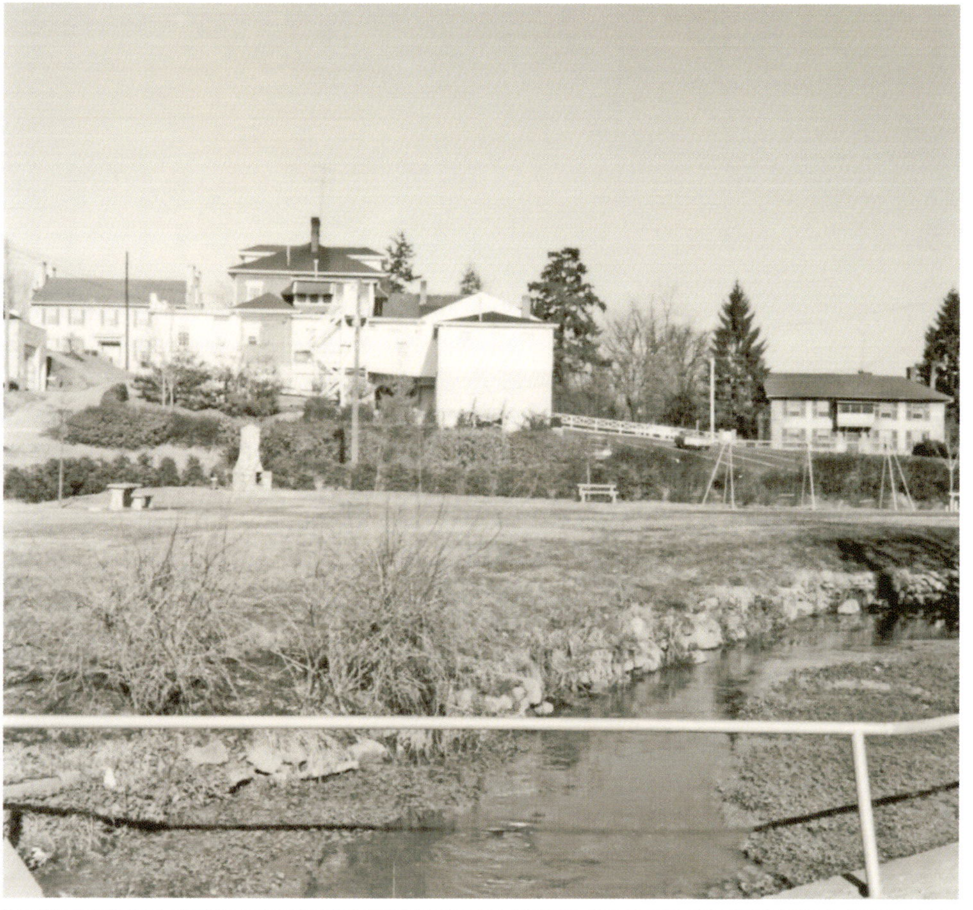

ABINGDON TOWN PARK. The 1967 photograph from the Town Park on Park Street into the eastern end of Main Street depicts a view that remains unchanged today. The James Longley/James K. Gibson house (1790) can be seen on the right. The rear of the Campbell (now Frost) Funeral Home is visible in the center. Town Creek is shown flowing in the foreground, just as it has since the earliest settlement days. (Peggy Johnson.)

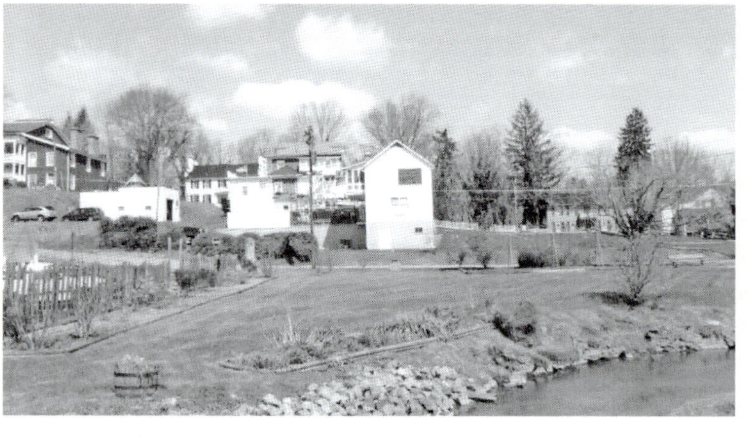

CHAPTER

CIVIC BUILDINGS, CHURCHES, SCHOOLS

VISITED, WORSHIPPED, AND LEARNED

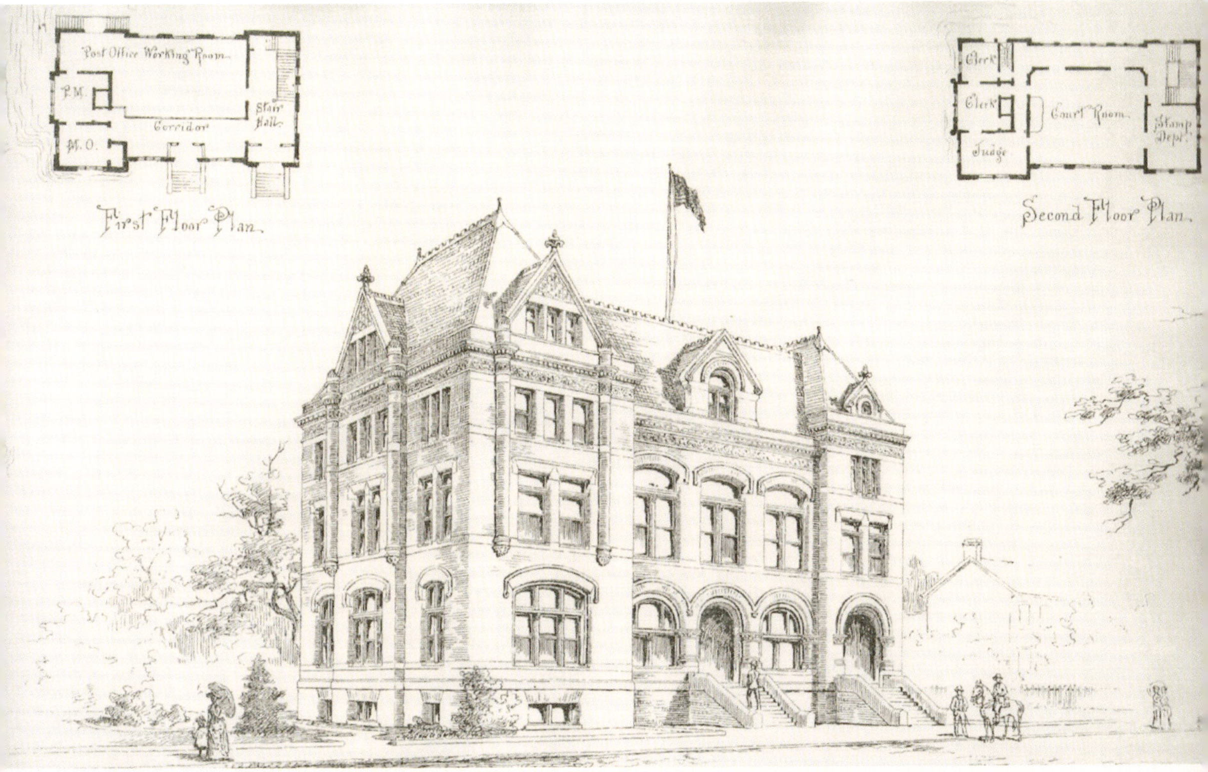

U.S. COURTHOUSE AND POST OFFICE. This 1875 sketch shows the imposing three-story brick building, which was completed in 1891 with a copper and slate roof, decorative crenellations, and Gothic details. Sadly, the building was demolished in the late 1950s in the name of progress. The new Abingdon Police Station on West Main Street was designed to resemble this architectural jewel of the town. The federal building was constructed on this empty lot in 1960. (Town of Abingdon.)

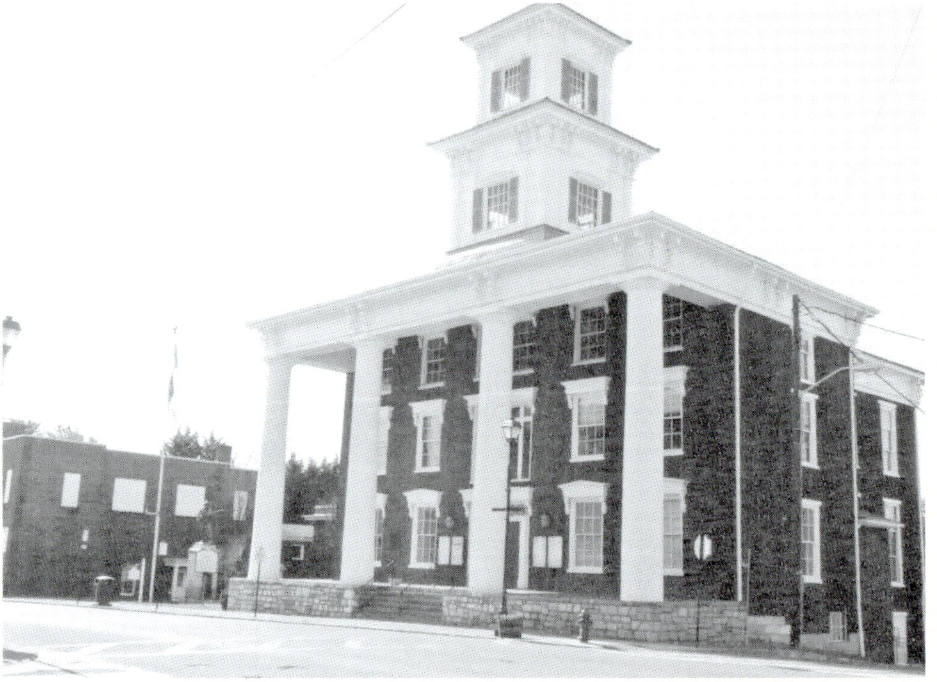

WASHINGTON COUNTY COURTHOUSE. The *c.* 1910 postcard at right shows the lovely Greek Revival–style Washington County Courthouse built in 1869 on Main Street. This is the fifth building to serve as the county's judicial seat. An annex was added to the courthouse, and the building still marks Abingdon as the county seat. (Peggy Johnson.)

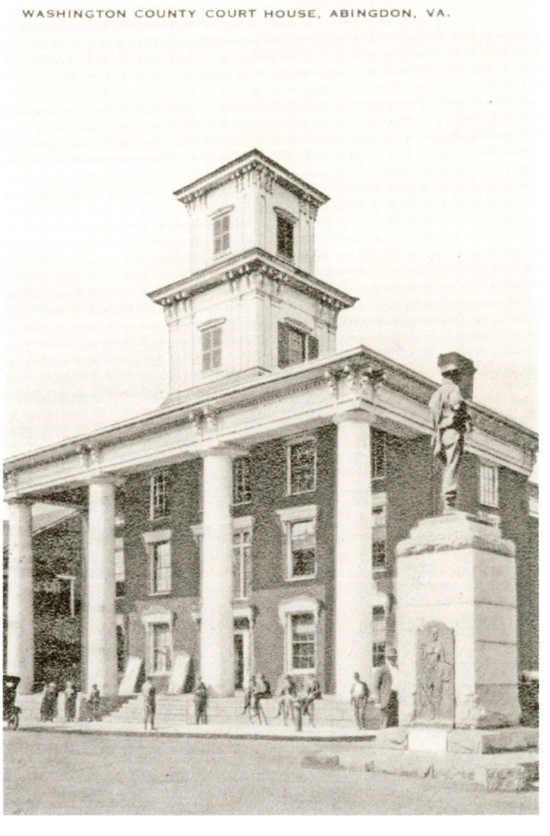

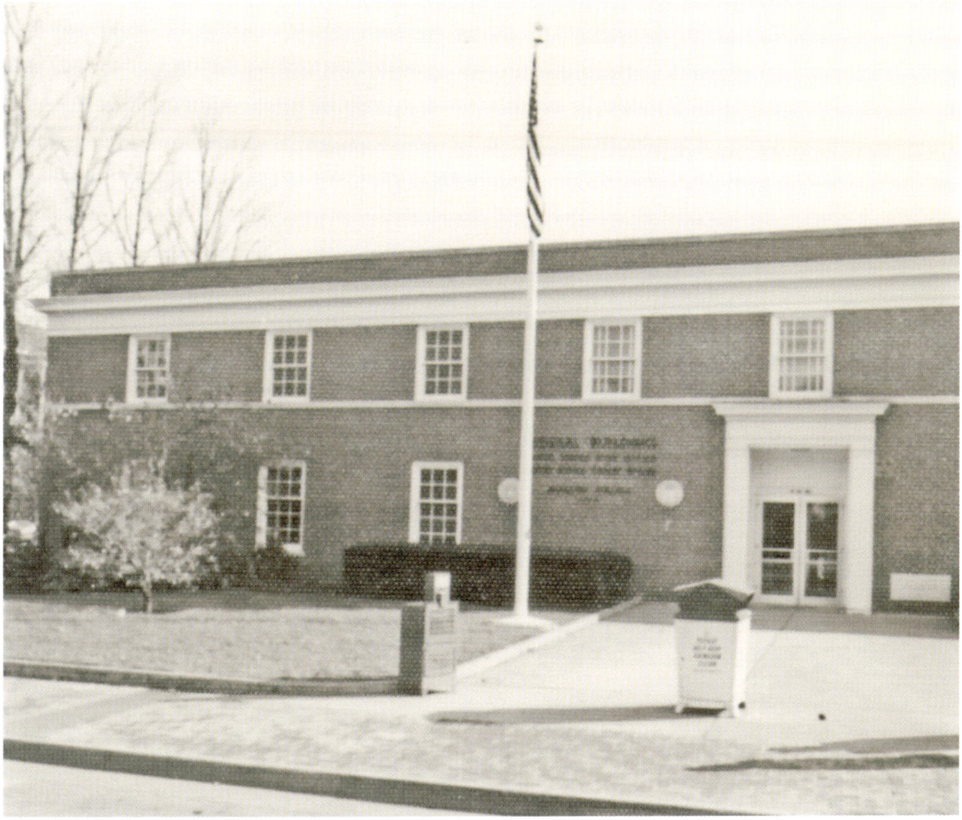

FEDERAL BUILDING. This building housed the U.S. Post Office at the corner of Cummings and Main Streets. It was built in 1960, replacing a stately two-story building that housed the federal courts and the post office until 1981. Today, the federal building (1960) has been returned to the lot's historic use as a federal courthouse. (Town of Abingdon.)

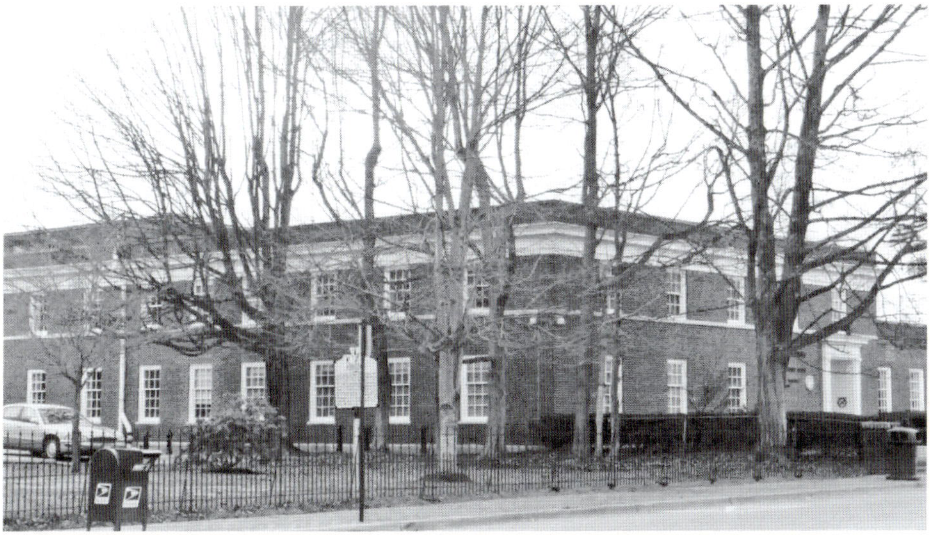

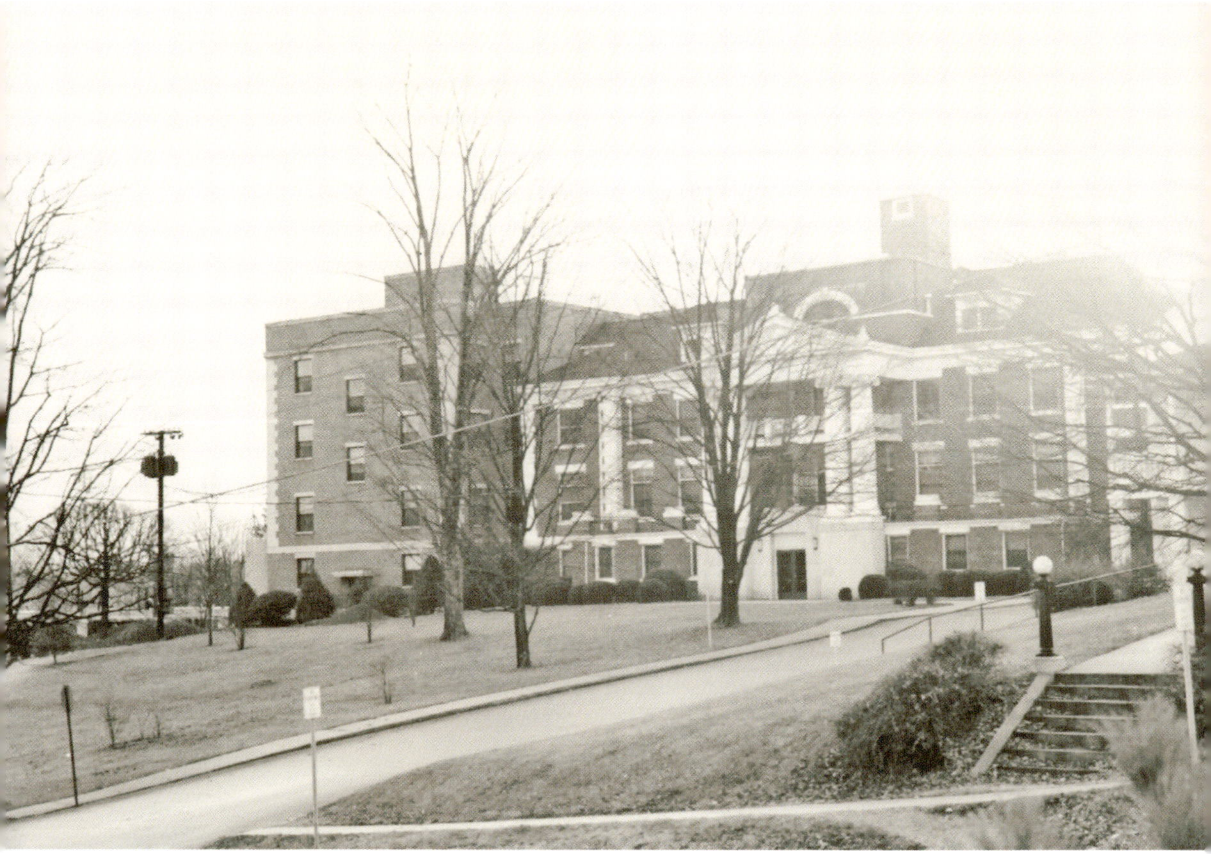

Johnston Memorial Hospital. The Johnston Memorial Hospital was constructed in 1919 and is still at the center of today's building. Abingdon's first hospital was built at this site in 1905 by Dr. E. T. Brady, but it was later demolished and replaced with the columned brick building. Unfortunately, the building has become outmoded for today's technology, and a new hospital is being built in Washington County. The future use of this building in downtown remains uncertain. (Peggy Johnson.)

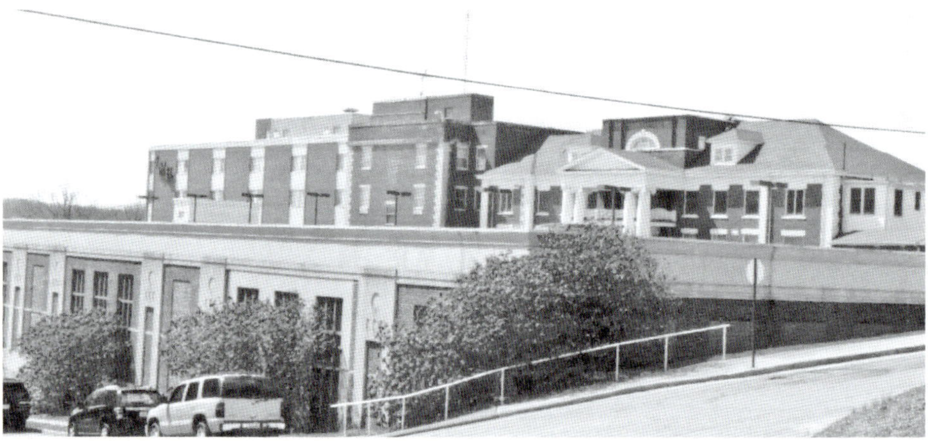

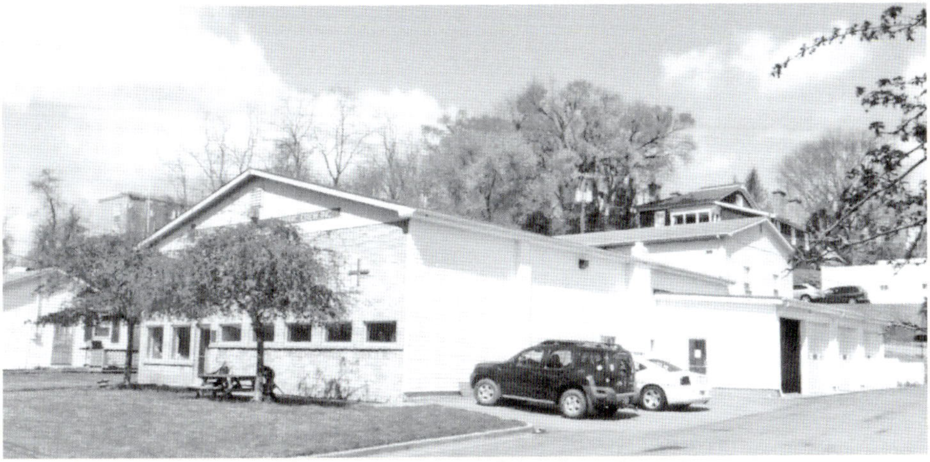

Washington County Life Saving Crew Building. This utilitarian building, shown in 1967, is located on Park Street and houses the dedicated Washington County Life Saving Crew. Built in the 1950s, this building has had several additions constructed to the rear and bays added for the ambulances. (Peggy Johnson.)

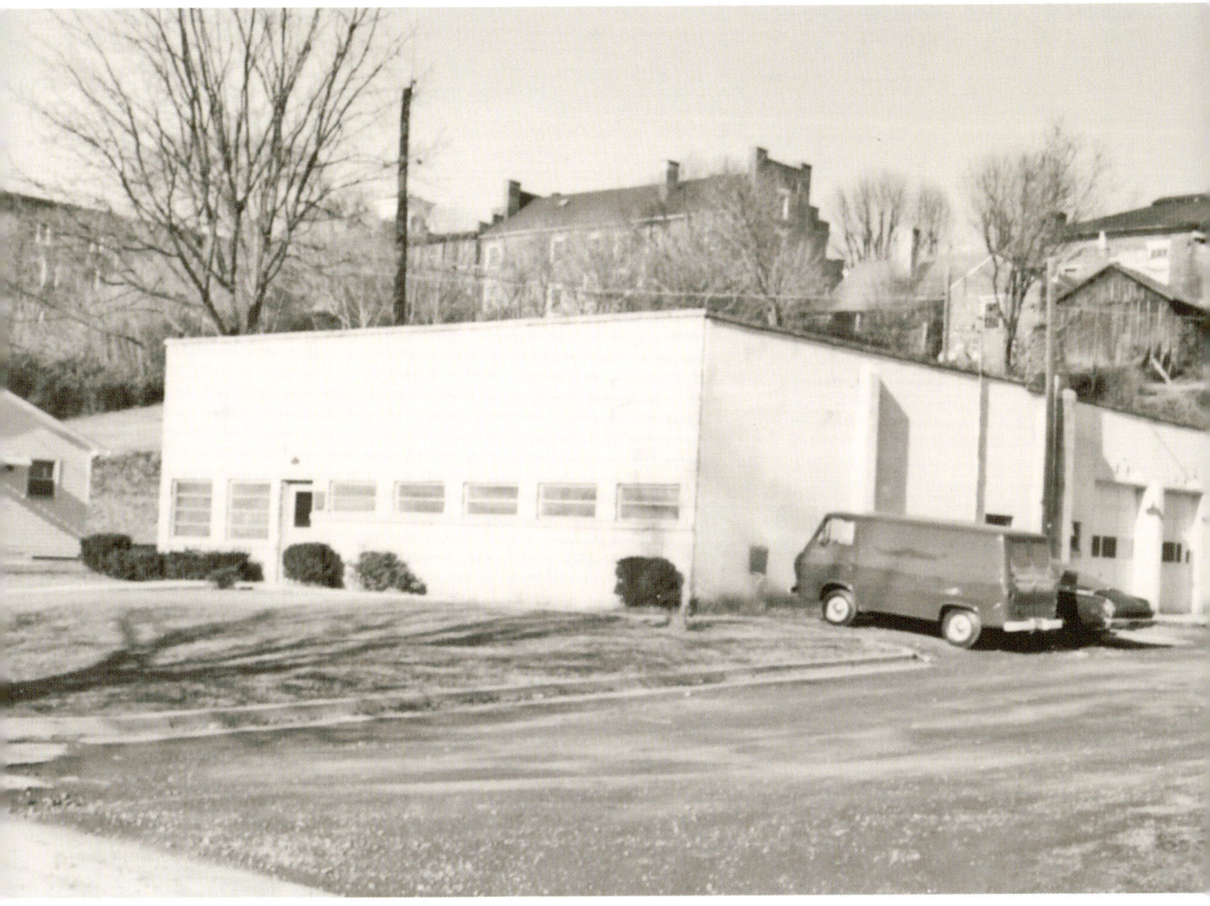

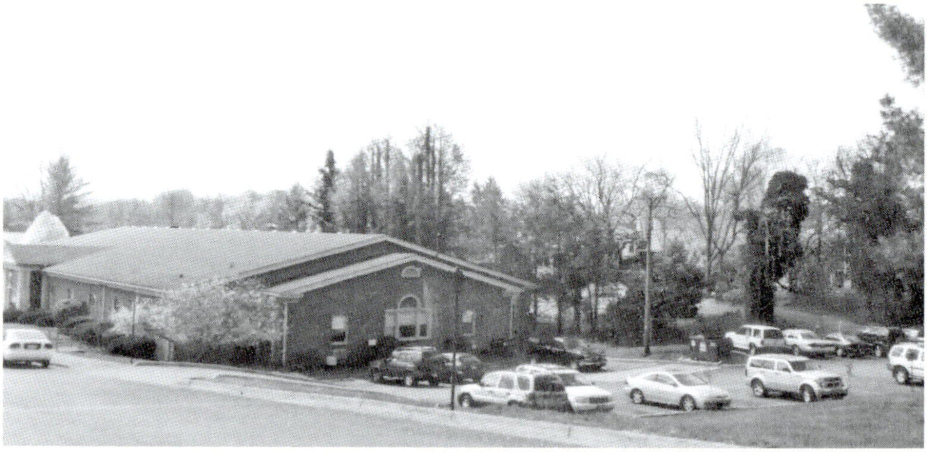

Abingdon Public School. Located on Oak Hill Street, the beautiful Abingdon Public School was built in 1892 with Italianate and Greek Revival details. Unfortunately, the building was torn down and replaced with Central Elementary School in the same location about 1925. Central School burned in 1964, and the Washington County Library (1975 to present) and its parking lot now occupy the lot. (Myra Worsham Martin.)

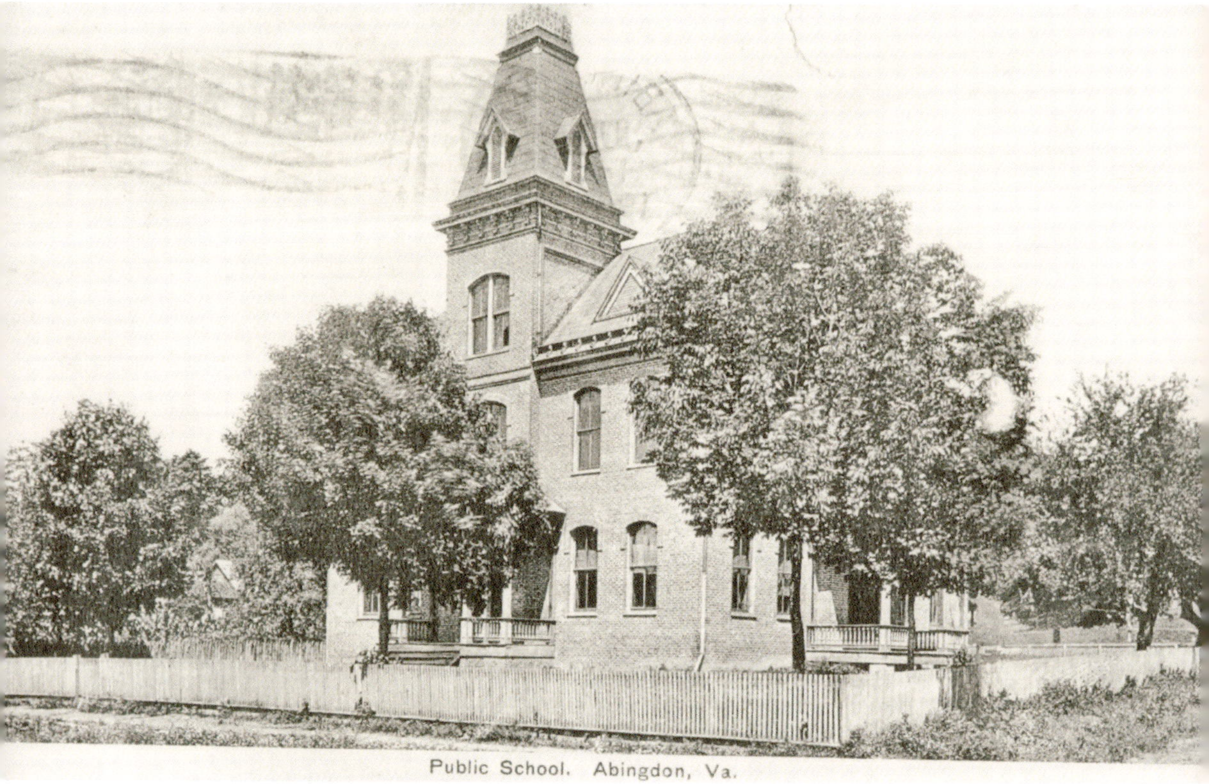

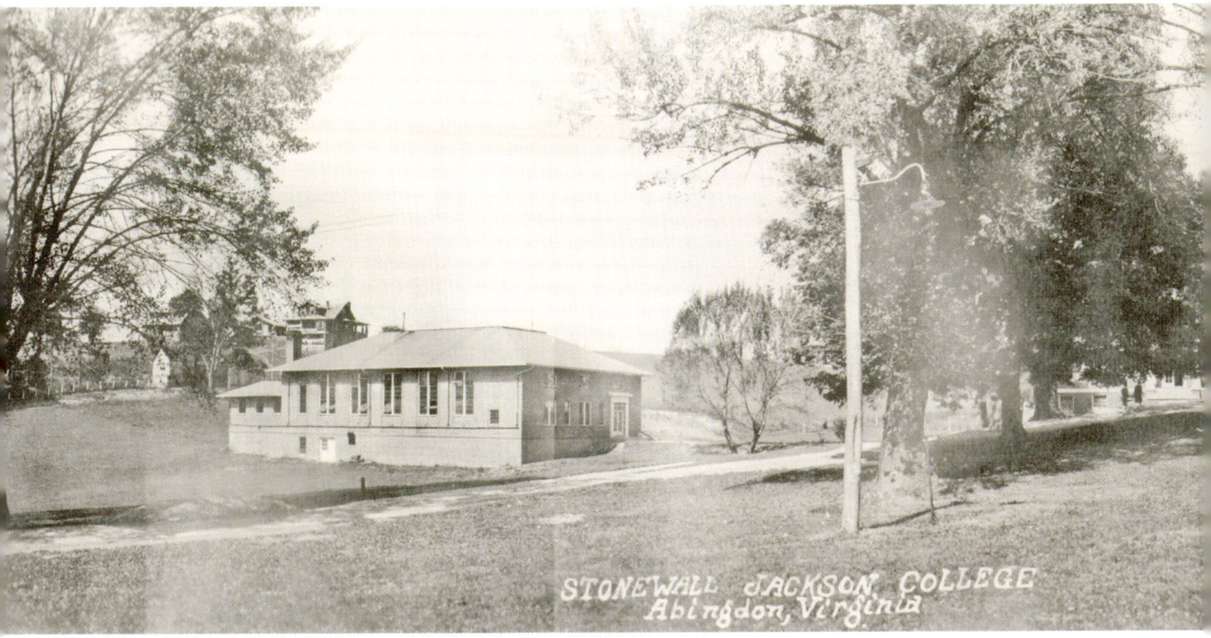

STONEWALL JACKSON COLLEGE: COURT HILL. The vintage photograph above is a section of a large early-20th-century panoramic view of the college. First located to the east of Martha Washington College, the school was founded in 1869 by the Sinking Spring Presbyterian Church as a female seminary. After a 1914 fire destroyed the buildings, a new campus was constructed on Court Hill, as shown in the modern image below. (Stephen Jett.)

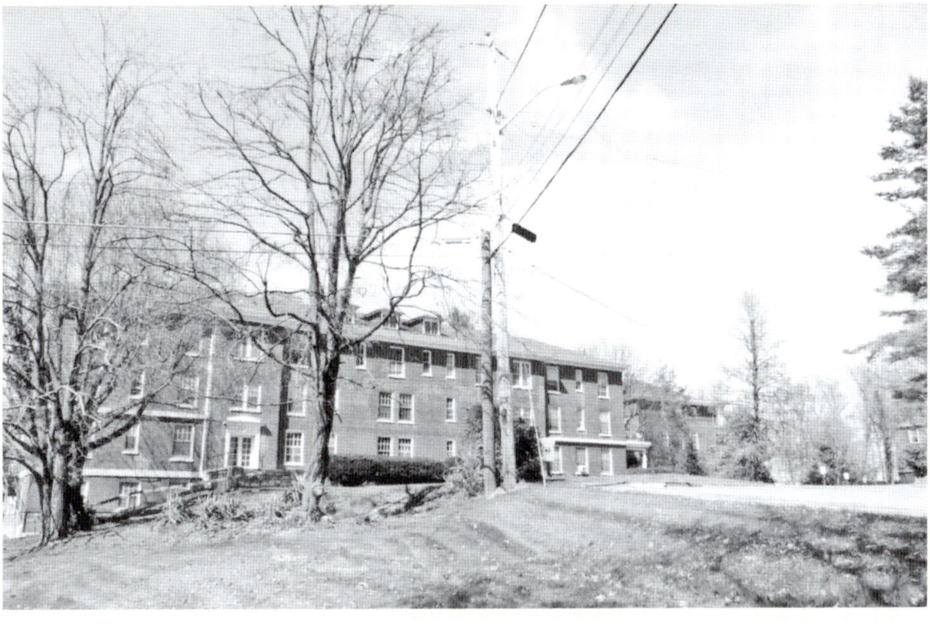

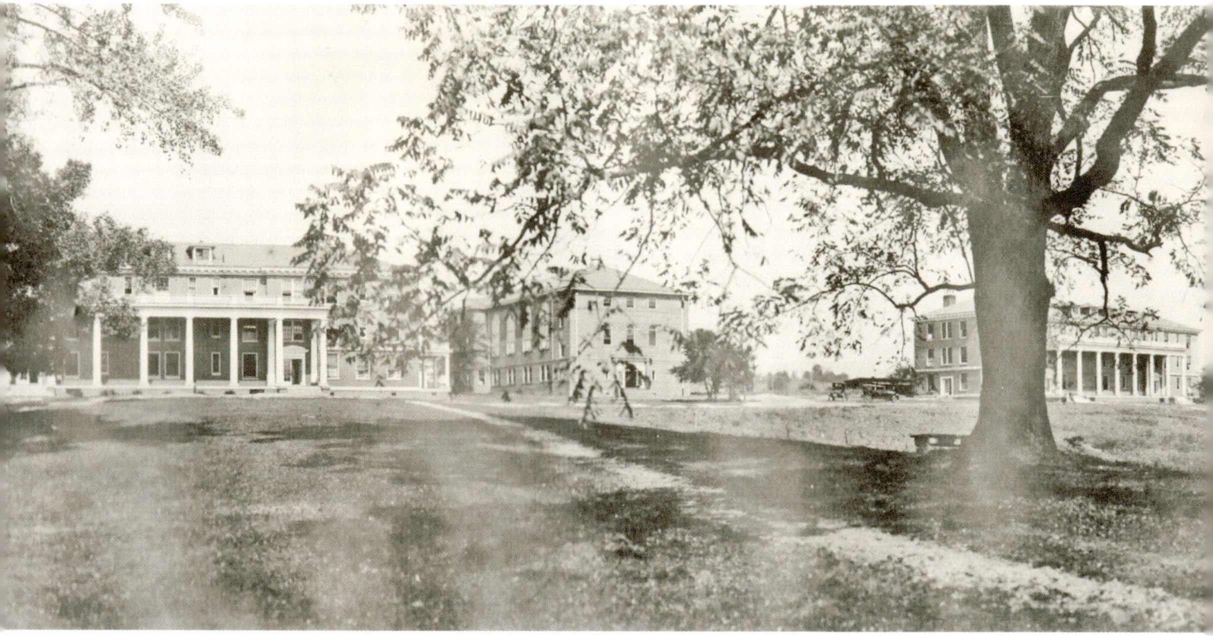

Stonewall Jackson College. The photograph above is the middle section of a panoramic view of the college. Stonewall Jackson College closed in 1930, but the three-story brick buildings have been used over the years for the Abingdon Academy, the Abingdon library (1954–1975), and a nursing school dormitory for Johnson Memorial Hospital. They are still used by the Barter Theatre and as apartments. (Stephen Jett.)

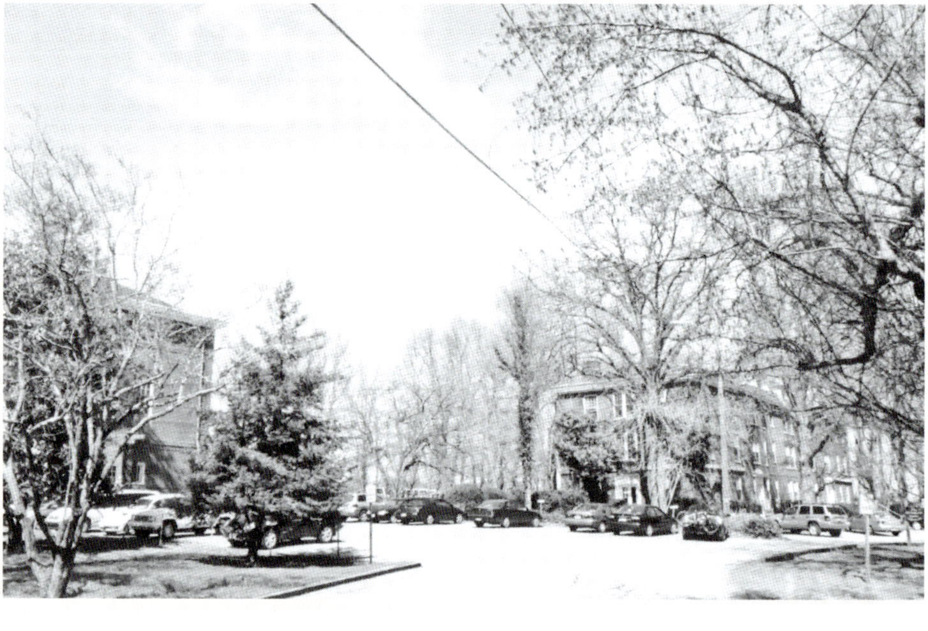

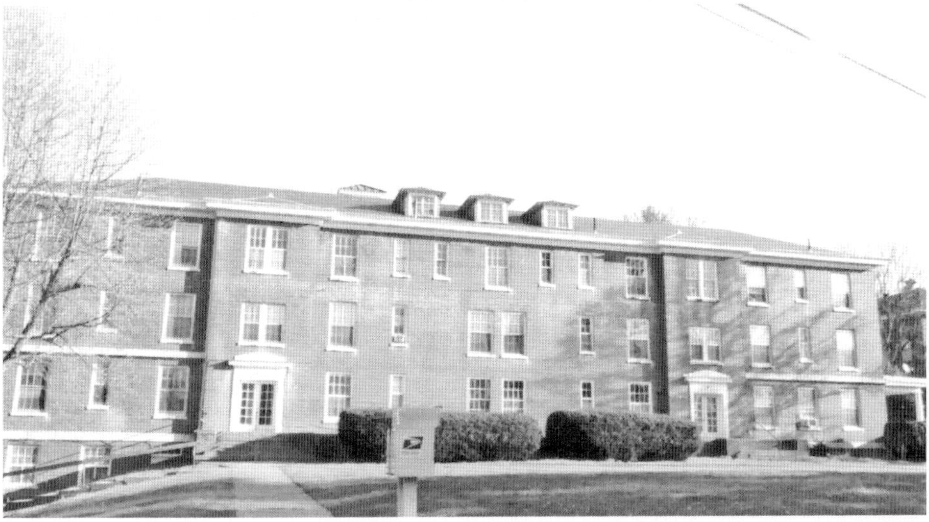

TORNADO DAMAGE TO STONEWALL JACKSON. A strong tornado tore through parts of Abingdon on March 4, 1944, and caused major damage to houses and buildings. Stonewall Jackson College, in its second location across from the hospital on Court Street, sustained major damage to several buildings. Abingdon Hall is shown below with damage to the facade. Columns were torn off, reportedly blown all the way to Valley Street. (Historical Society of Washington County.)

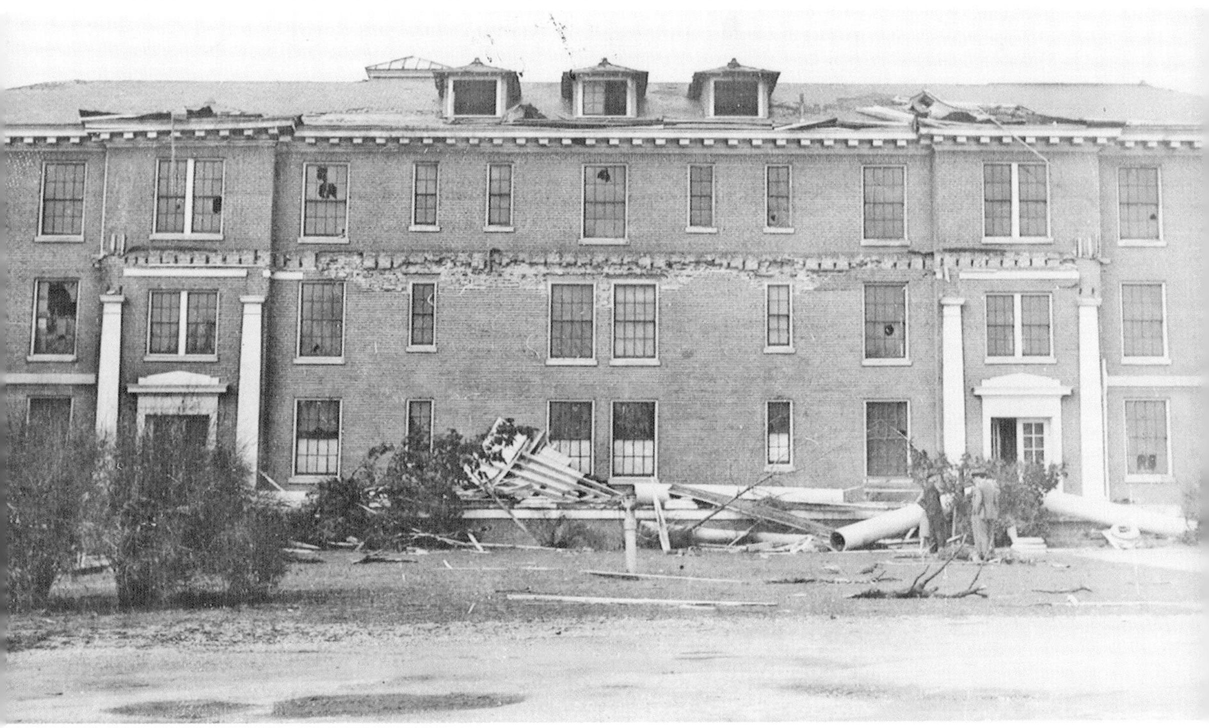

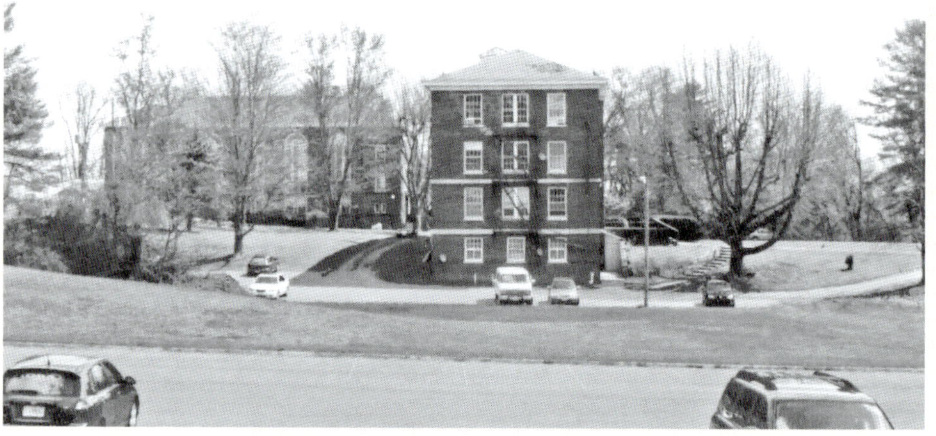

Stonewall Jackson College, 1966. These photographs of the Stonewall Jackson College buildings show the adaptive reuses of these buildings. Abingdon Hall (1921), to the left, was used as the Washington County Library for many years; McMillan Hall (1916), the center building, was used for the Johnston Memorial School of Nursing dormitory; and Montgomery Hall (1921), in the background, has been used by the Barter Theatre. Today, the Barter Theatre's scene shop and apartment rentals occupy these buildings. (Peggy Johnson.)

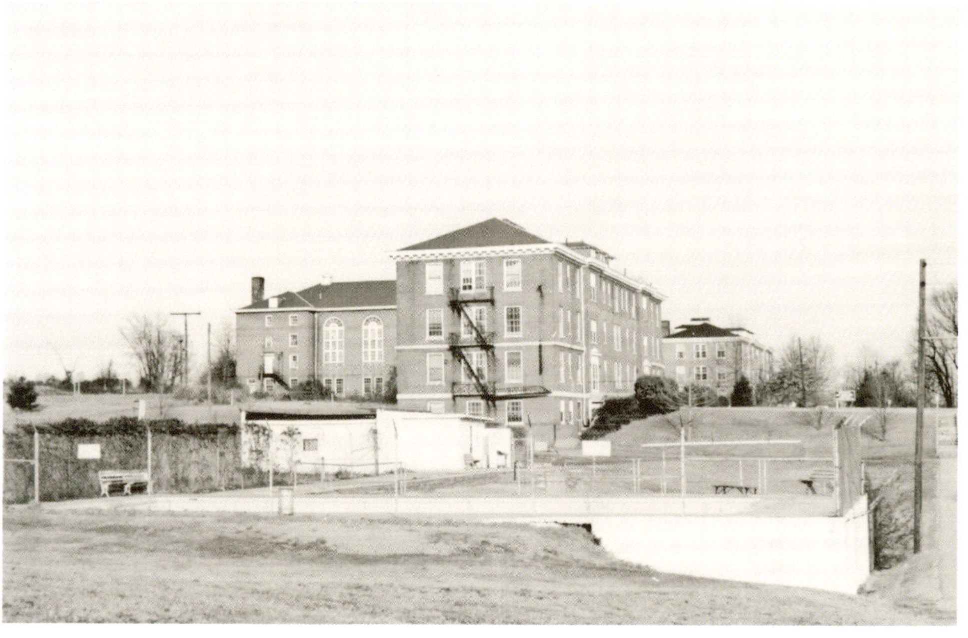

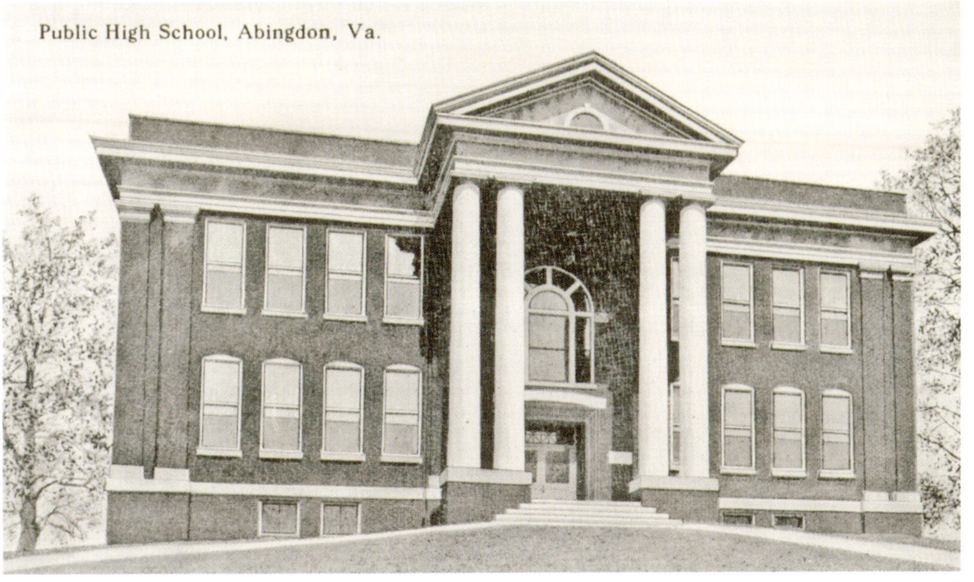

WILLIAM KING HIGH SCHOOL. The William King High School was built in 1913 on top of a hill overlooking downtown Abingdon and replaced the earlier Abingdon Academy on the lot. The school served students until Abingdon High School was built in 1959 on the eastern end of town. Comparing the early-20th-century postcard above and the modern image below shows few changes in its appearance, although it was renovated several years ago and houses the William King Regional Arts Center today. (Myra Worsham Martin.)

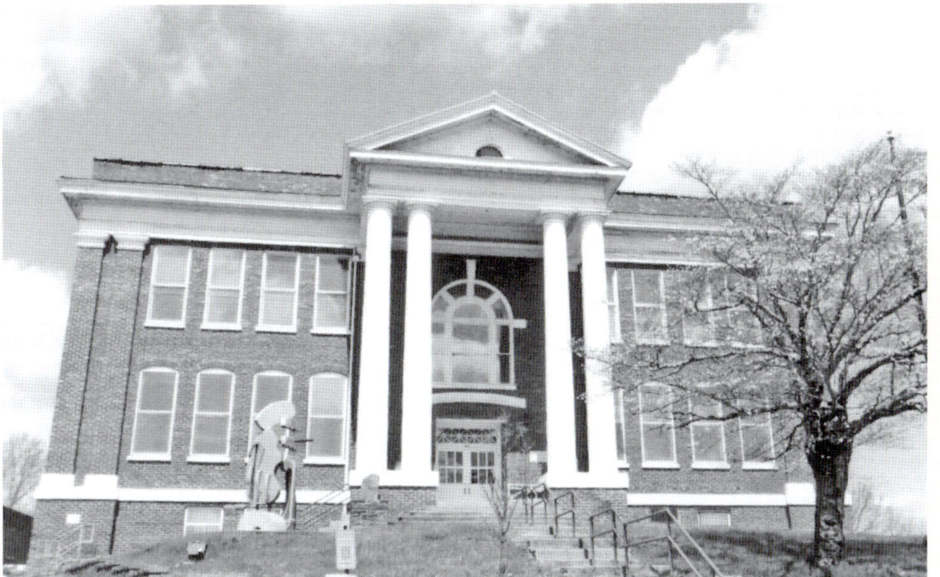

ABINGDON UNITED METHODIST CHURCH. Shown at right in an early-20th-century postcard, the Abingdon United Methodist Church still graces Main Street and has retained its historic appearance. Built in 1884, the church incorporates Gothic details as well as Greek Revival. The congregation first met in a log meetinghouse in the 1770s, and the church was originally formed as part of the Methodist Episcopal Church South. (Myra Worsham Martin.)

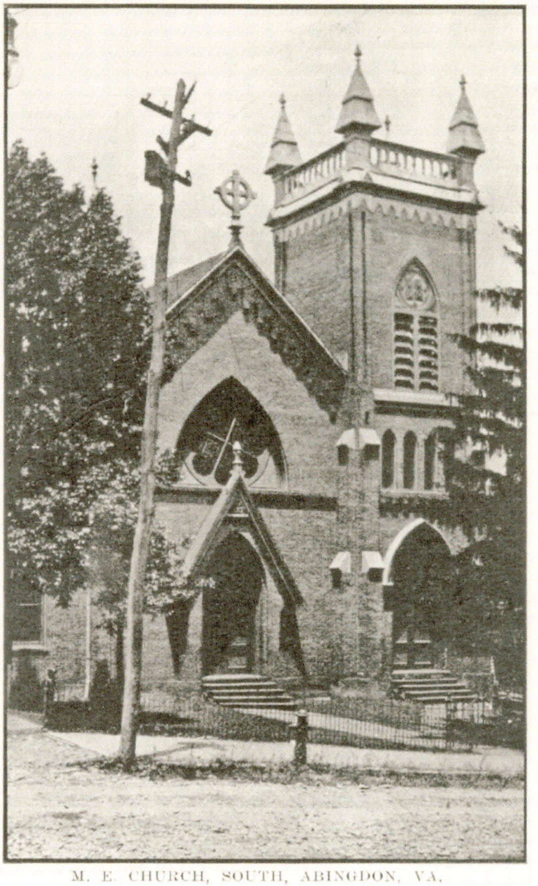

M. E. CHURCH, SOUTH, ABINGDON, VA.

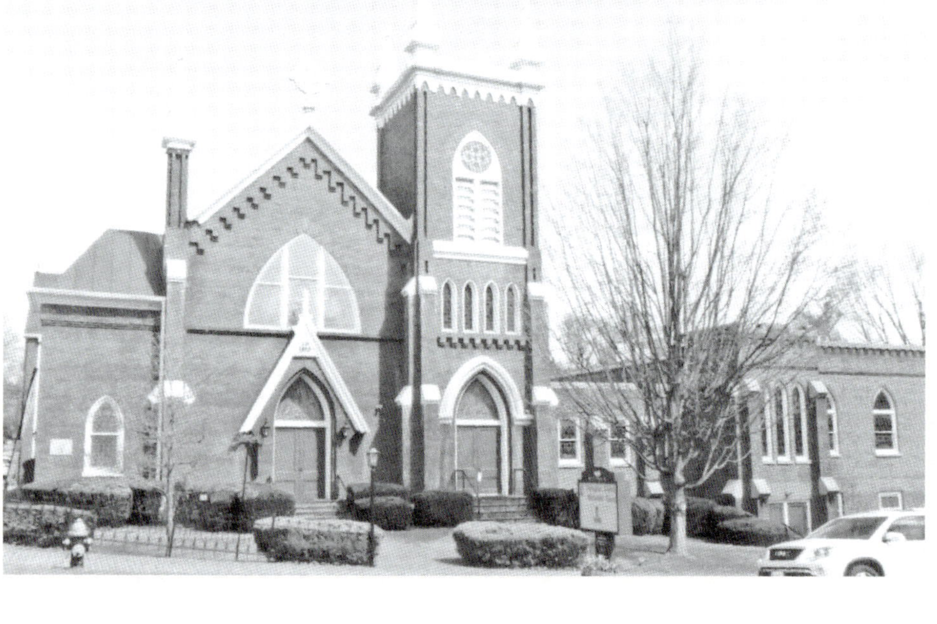

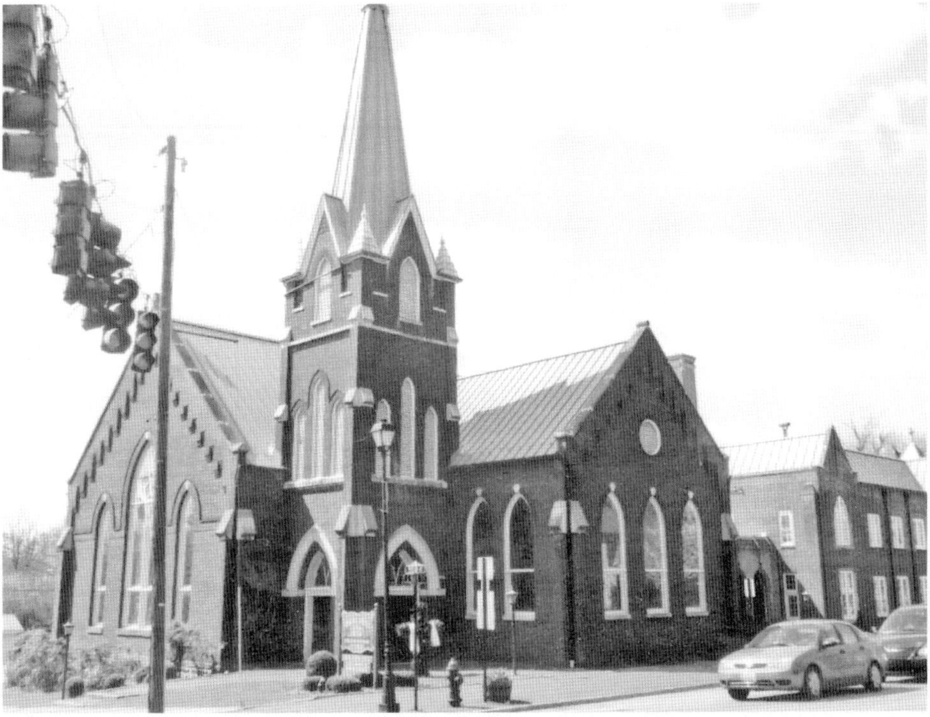

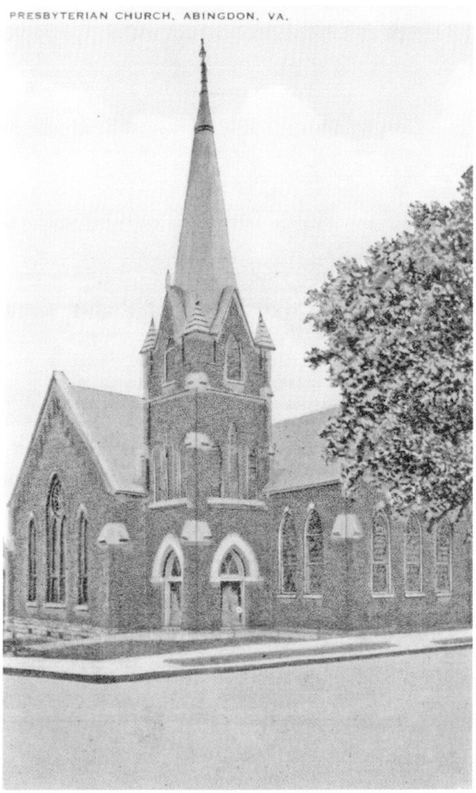

SINKING SPRING PRESBYTERIAN CHURCH. The early-1900s-postcard at left shows the lovely church built in 1889 at the corner of Main and Pecan Streets to replace several earlier churches. This faithful congregation is one of the earliest in the region, having organized before 1772 with its first resident minister, Rev. Charles Cummings. The third church was constructed in 1832 and now houses the Barter Theatre. The steeple stands out as one of the taller structures in town. (Myra Worsham Martin.)

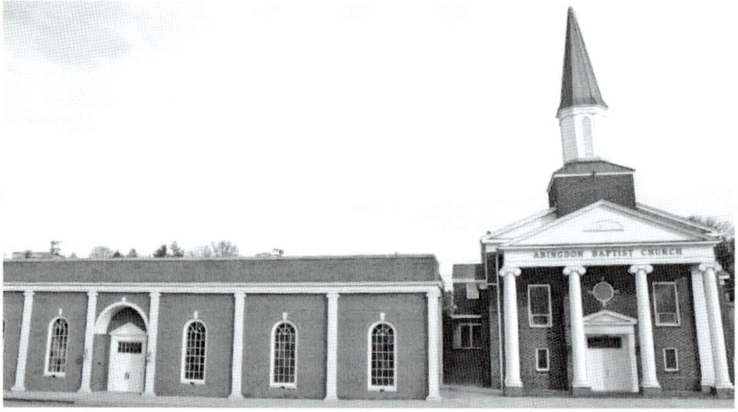

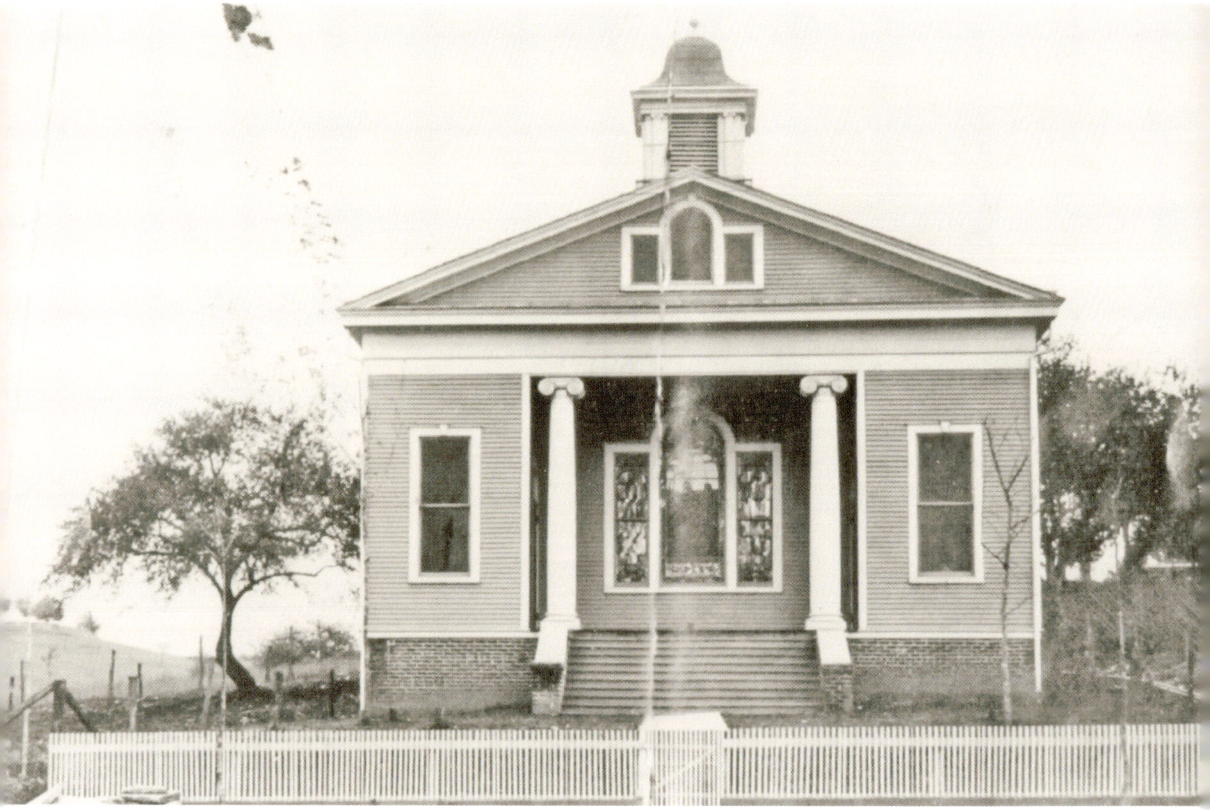

ABINGDON BAPTIST CHURCH. The Abingdon Baptist Church was built in 1908 on West Main Street near today's Abingdon Police Station. The Reverend H. W. Bellamy served as the first pastor. A brick veneer was added later, and the church grew into the stately two-story brick building with bell tower that is seen today. The building to the left was previously a car dealership, but the church acquired it for its use. (Then, Irene Meade Johnson; now, Fred Tweed.)

CHAPTER

BUSINESSES

Shopped and Traded

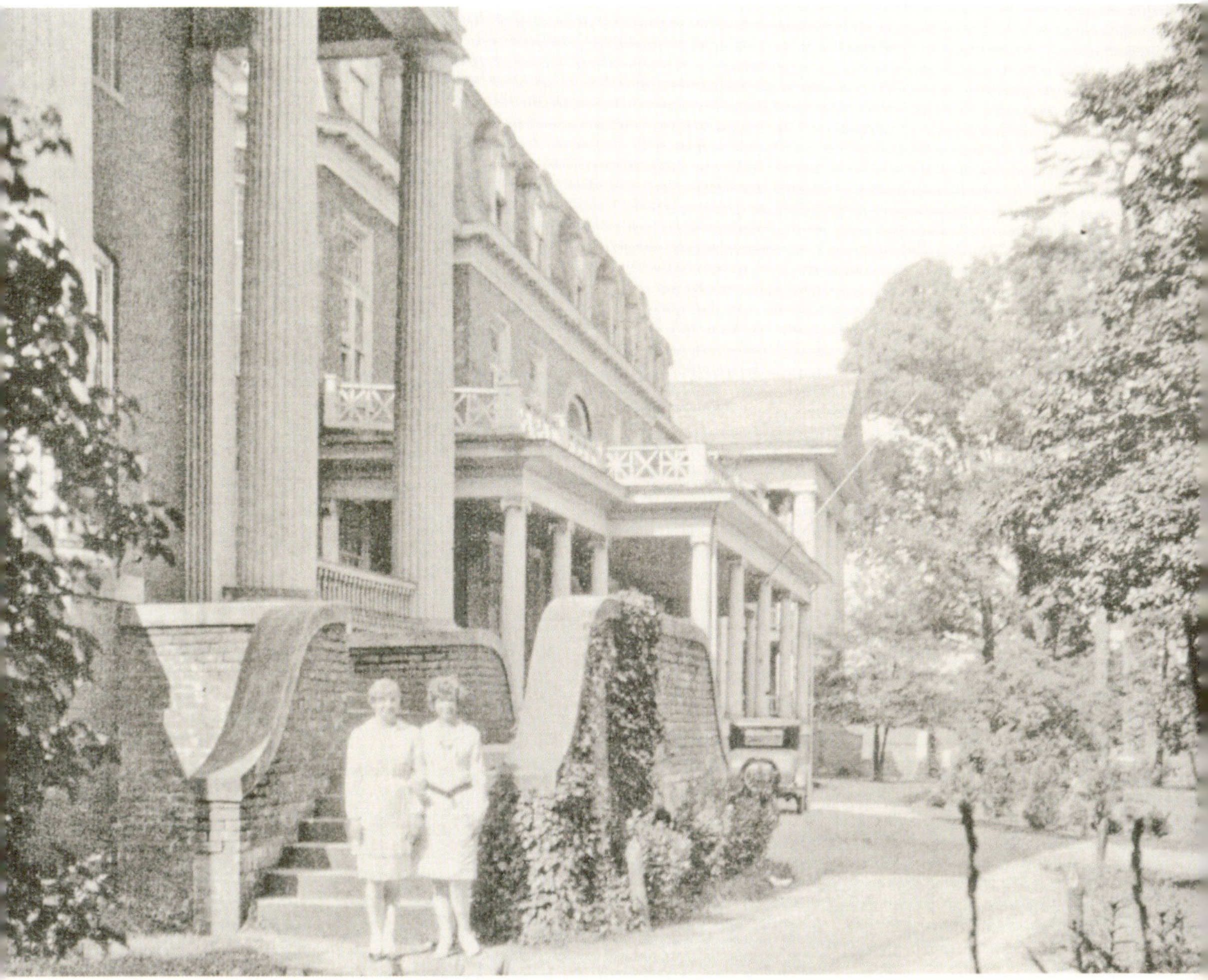

Martha Girls around 1920. Sporting fashionable 1920s bobs, these two lovely women pose in front of Litchfield Hall's stairs at Martha Washington College. These ladies may either be students at Martha Washington (1860–1919) or simply visitors. The historic integrity of this stately building has been well preserved. (Edith Maiden Hatcher.)

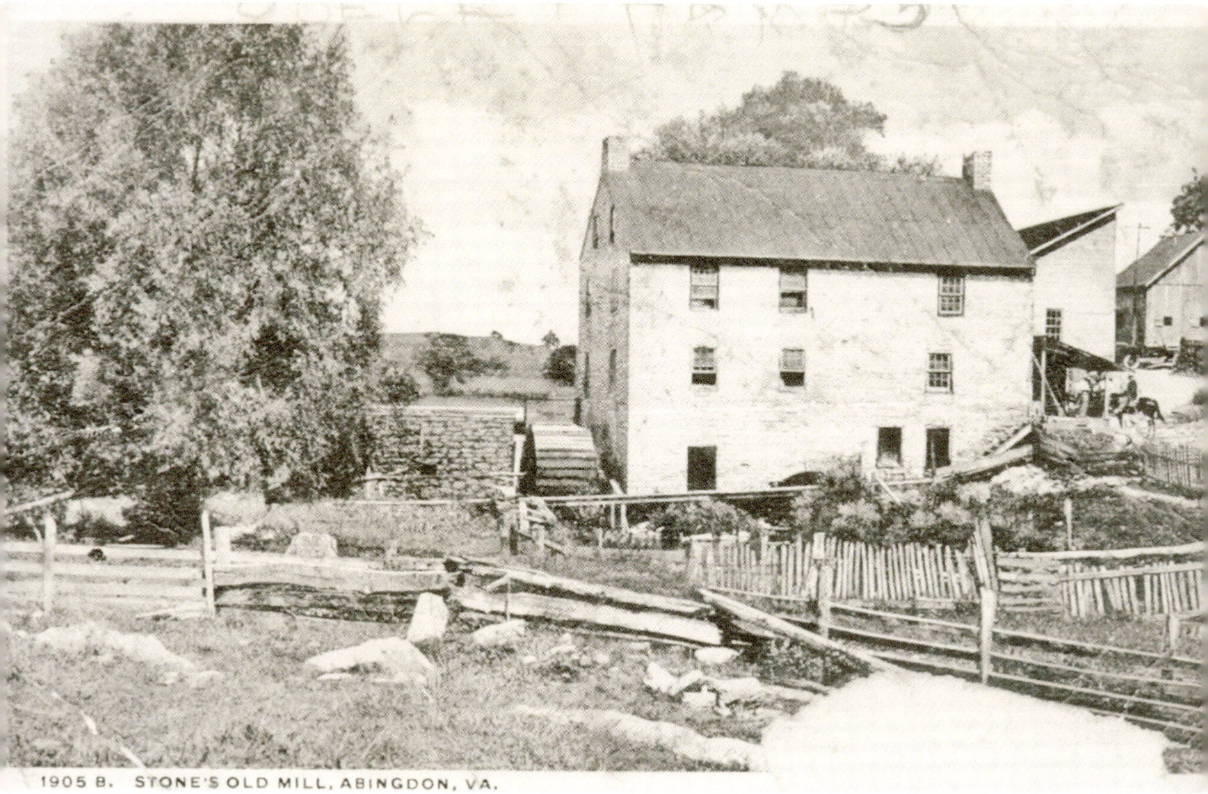

STONE MILL. Known as the Old Stone Mill, this two-story mill was positioned conveniently along Stone Mill Road. Many gristmills were built from the late 1700s to early 1900s to grind the wheat and corn grown in this fertile river valley. This fulling mill was built before 1815 to process woolen textiles. Destroyed by fire in 1964, only limestone foundation sections and parts of the raceway remain, visible from the recently completed Overmountain Victory National Historic Trail. (Garrett Jackson.)

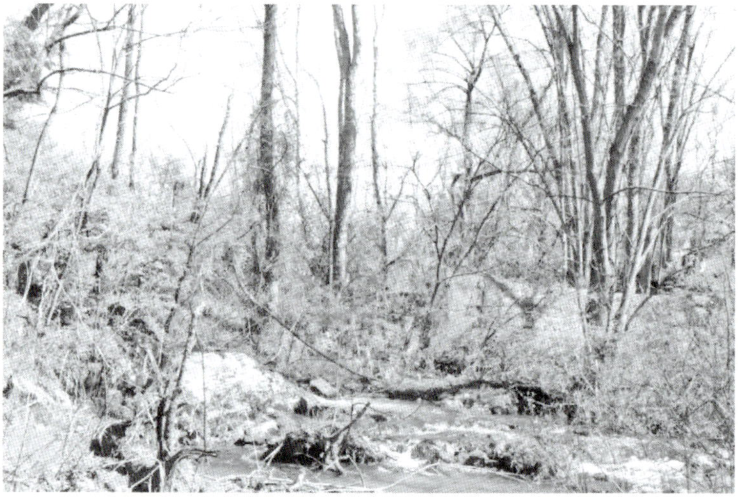

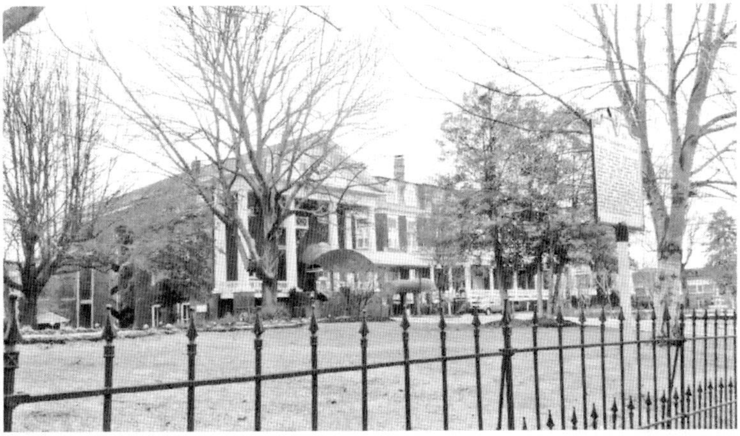

MARTHA WASHINGTON INN. The Martha Washington Inn and Litchfield Hall, located on Main Street, appear in the early-20th-century photograph below. Preston Hall was built in the Federal style in 1832 as a private residence, and later, the building was used for a private girls' school, the Martha Washington College (1860–1919), with students from throughout the southeast. The buildings have been a luxury hotel for many years. A brick entryway, no longer there, is visible on the front of the hall. (Garrett Jackson.)

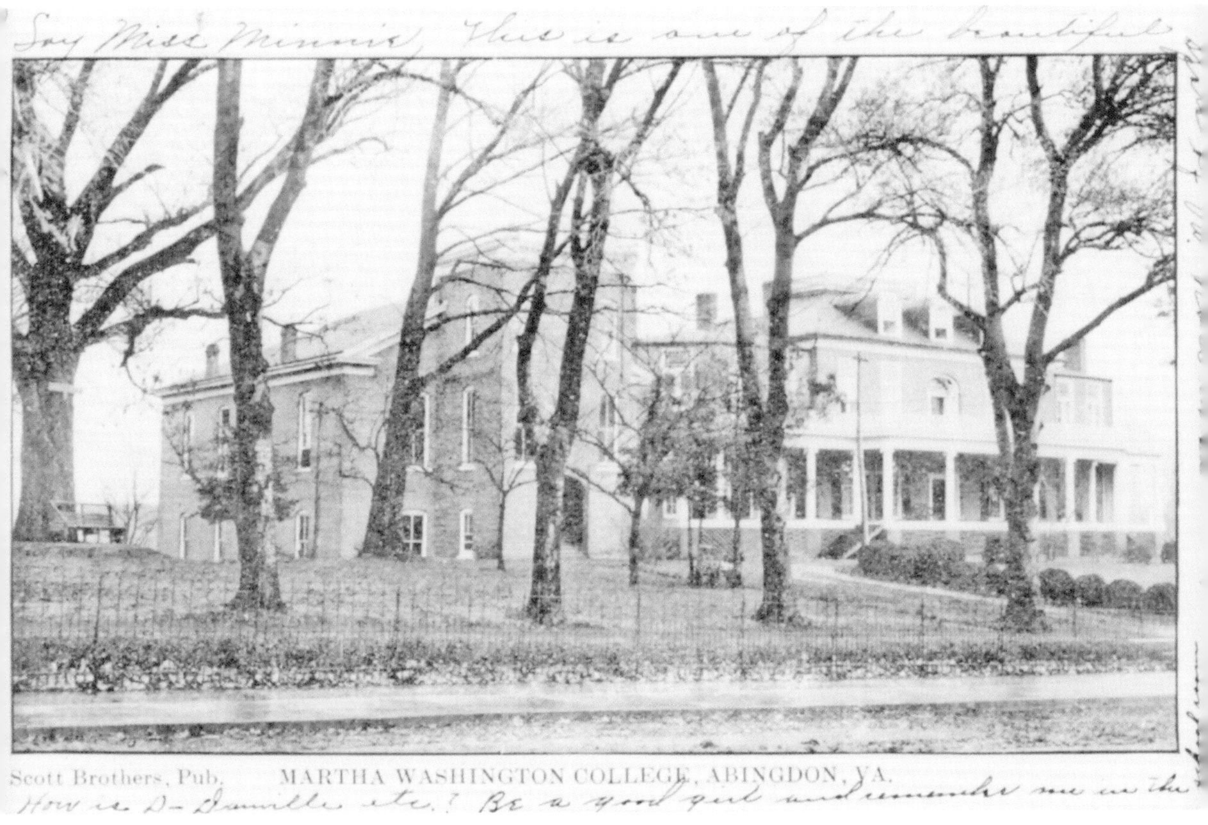

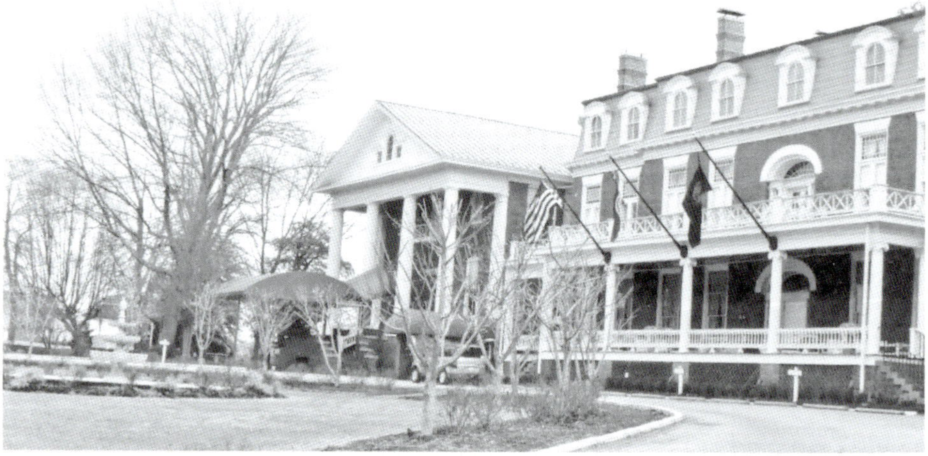

Litchfield Hall. Witness to years of town history, Litchfield Hall, at the venerable Martha Washington Inn, stands as the left wing of the hotel. The center section of the existing building was constructed in 1832 as a house, then with side buildings added became Martha Washington College (1860–1919), and finally a hotel. This grandest dame of Abingdon is on the exclusive Historic Hotels of America listing and includes conference facilities, a spa, and recreational areas. (Martha Washington Inn.)

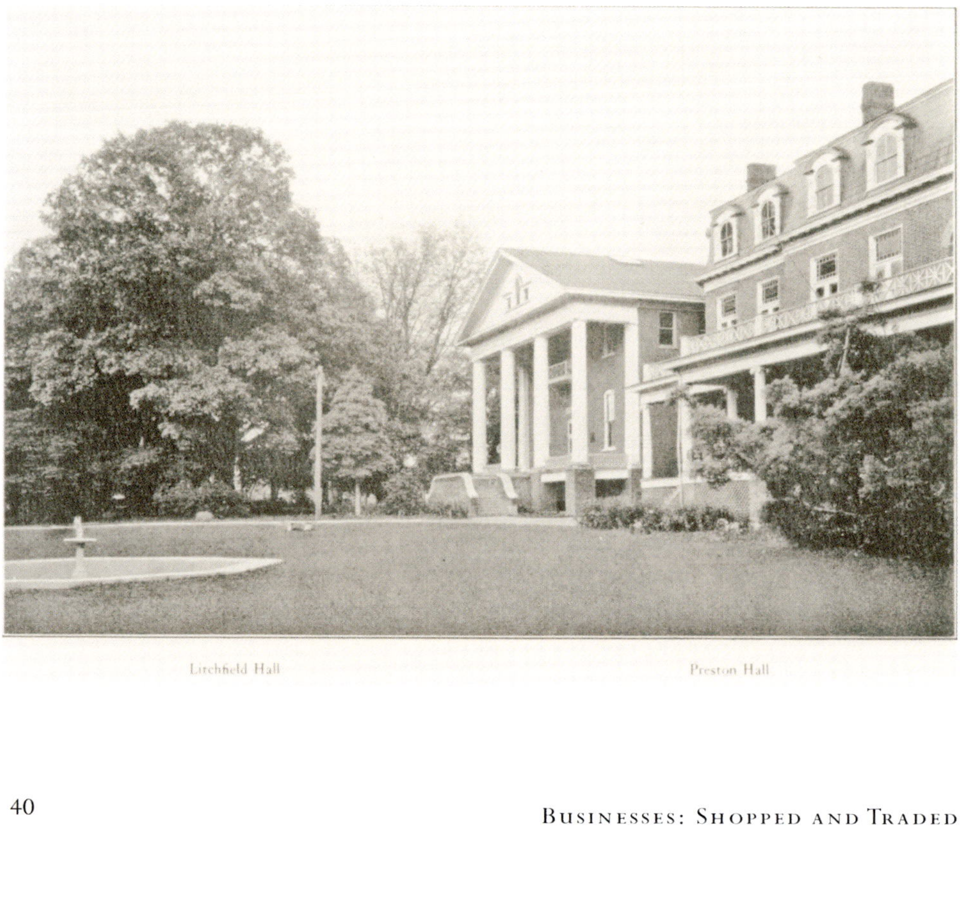

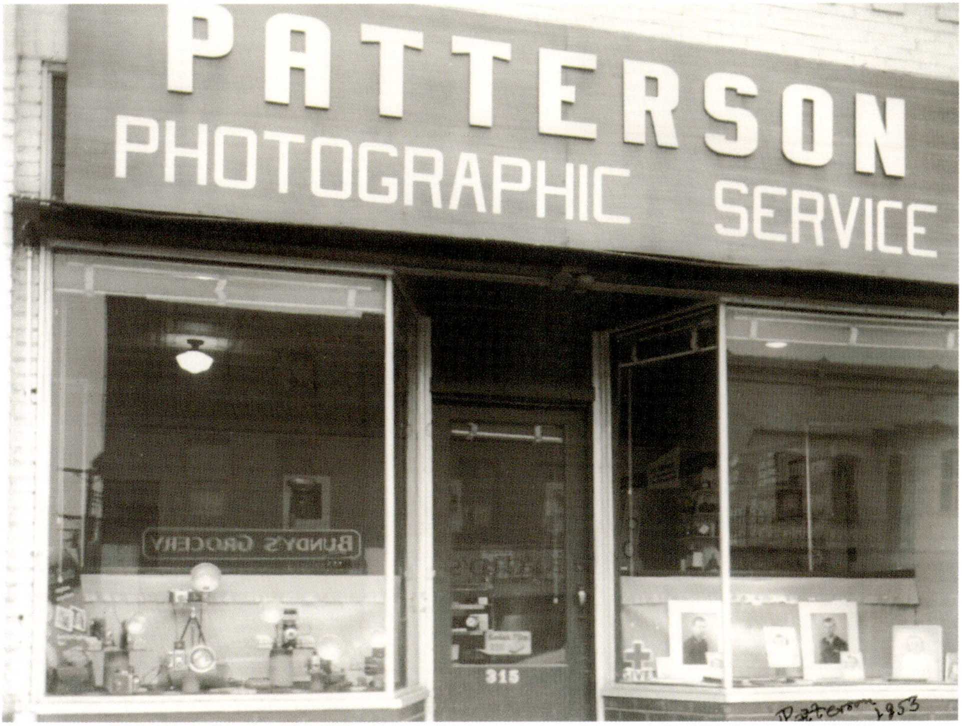

PATTERSON PHOTOGRAPHIC STUDIO. Douglas Patterson built his photography studio here in 1960, replacing the I. B. Wells home demolished in 1959. Adjacent businesses included the Abingdon Lodge #48 and Arnolds' Jewelry store. Patterson, a well-known portrait and commercial photographer, ran his busy downtown studio for many years. He took many photographs of Abingdon and the area and willingly shared them with the author and others. He died on July 3, 2010, leaving a noble legacy. (Courtesy Douglas Patterson.)

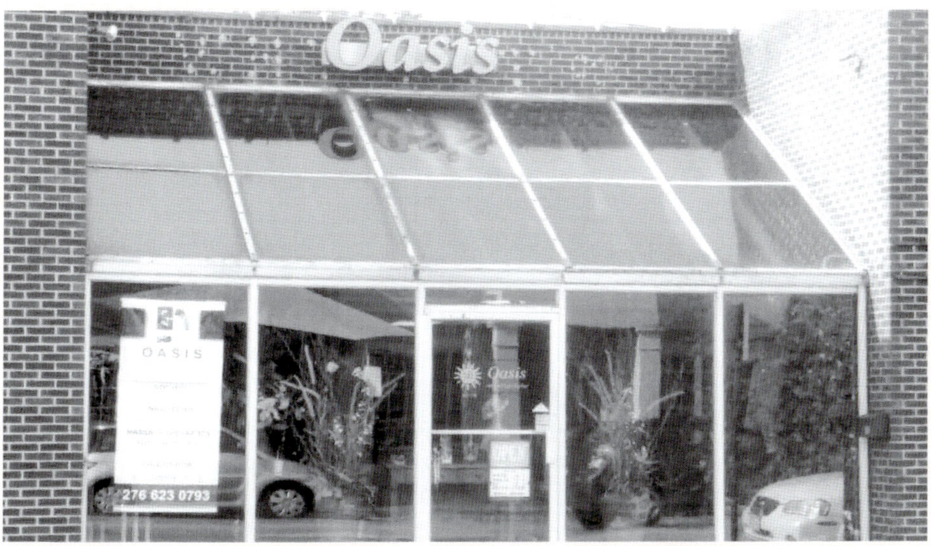

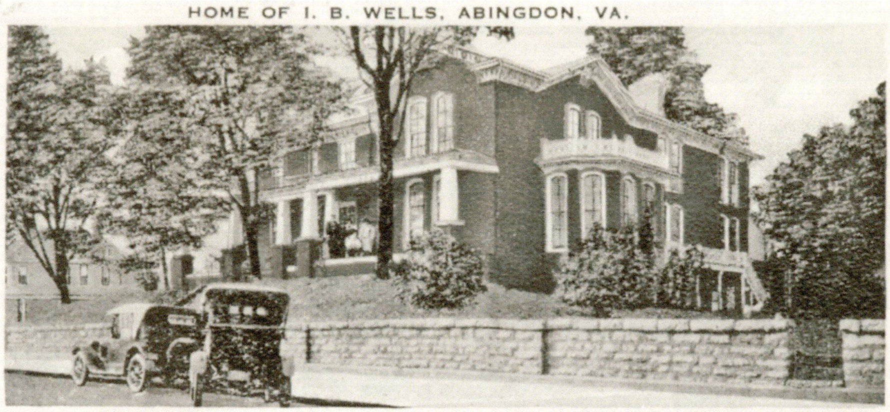

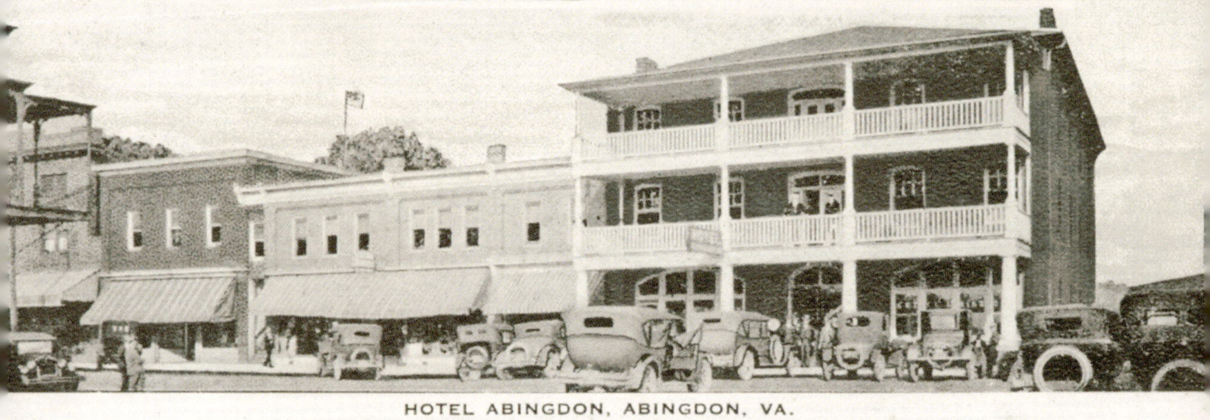

HOTEL ABINGDON. Shown in the 1920s postcard above are, from left to right, the Scott building (1913), Bell/Rice building (1909), West End Pharmacy (1901), Hotel Abingdon (1885), and the home of I. B. Wells, the hotel manager. First the Hattie House Hotel, the brick building later became Hotel Abingdon, advertising 40 rooms, electric lights, steam heat, and telephone connections. The hotel was quite busy with its position near the Abingdon Depot. The building is now occupied by a commercial store, while the other buildings have been demolished. (Edith Maiden Hatcher.)

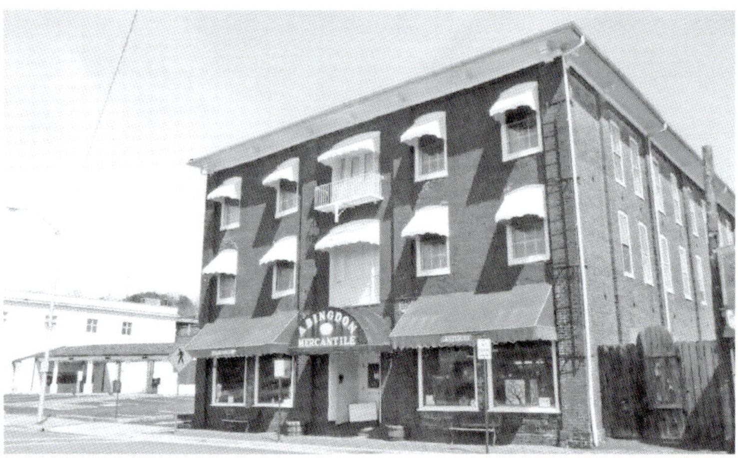

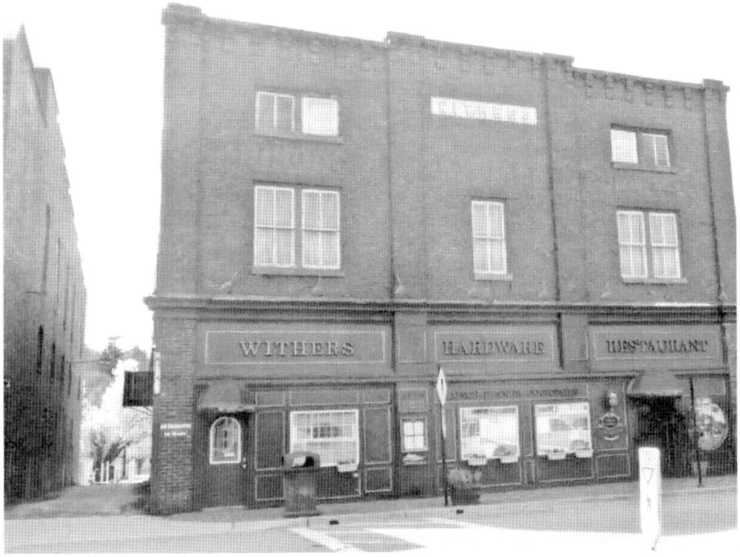

SCHAFFER-PRICE HARDWARE. Shown below in the late 1950s, the Schaffer-Price Hardware Company was a longstanding downtown business, preceded on this lot by a hardware store and stable that burned in the 1914 fire. Occupied by Withers Hardware and Hagy and McChesney jewelry store, it was a favorite destination for local men, and many remember sidling up to its long wooden counter. The counter is still there and is used for a bar in a restaurant. (Peggy Johnson.)

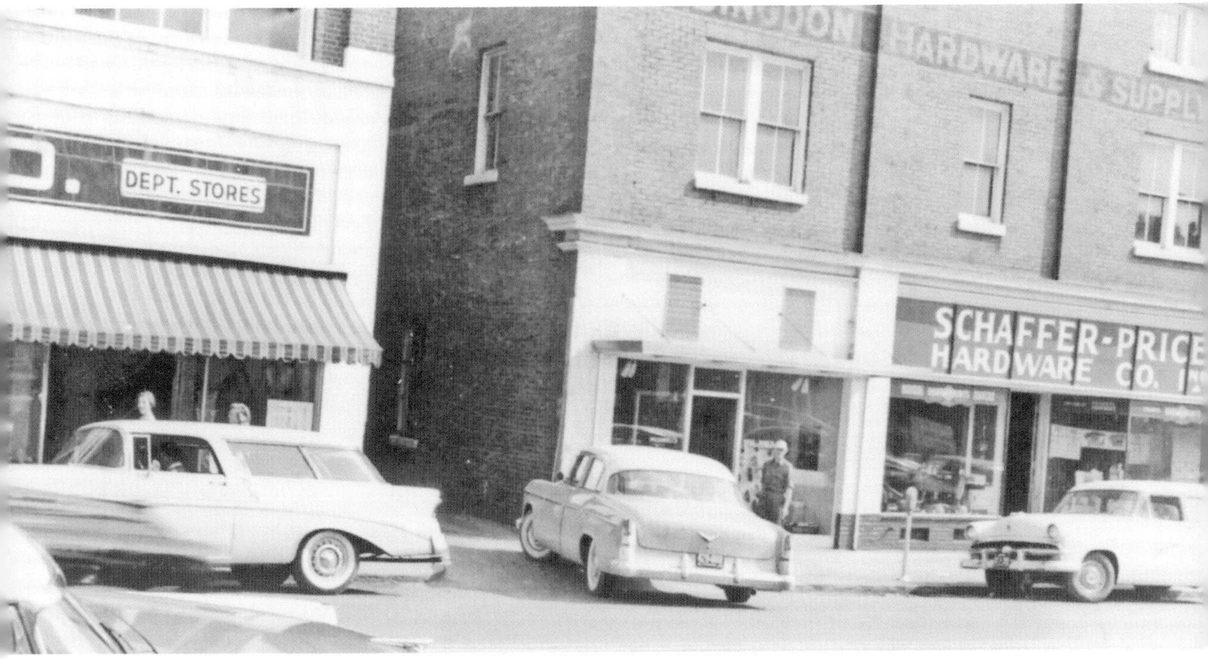

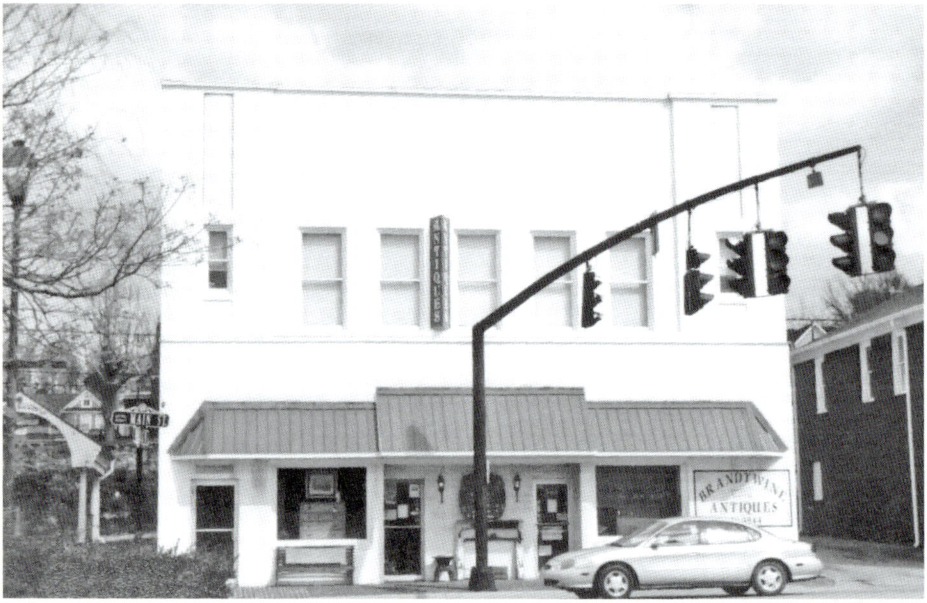

CITIZENS BANK/PEOPLE'S DRUG. Citizens Bank and Trust Company had this building constructed at the intersection of Wall and Main Streets in 1908 and clad with light brown brick, providing a contrast to the dominant red brick color in town. After 1923, the bank became Peoples Drug Store, and after 1935, another drugstore business occupied the building. Downtown once supported several drugstores and soda fountains. The building houses an antique store today. (Peggy Johnson.)

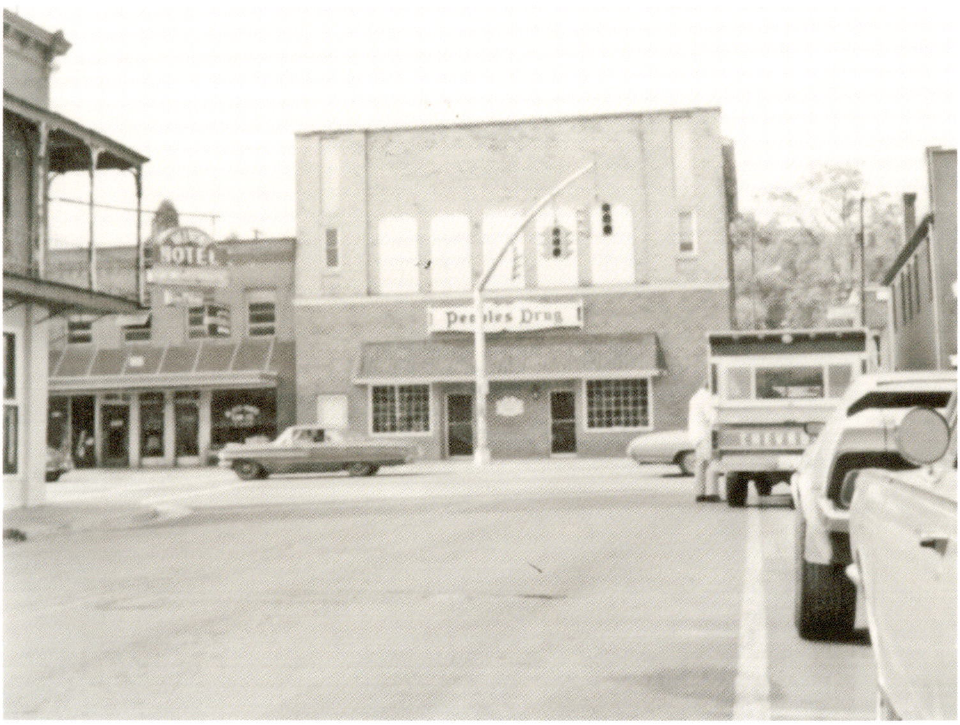

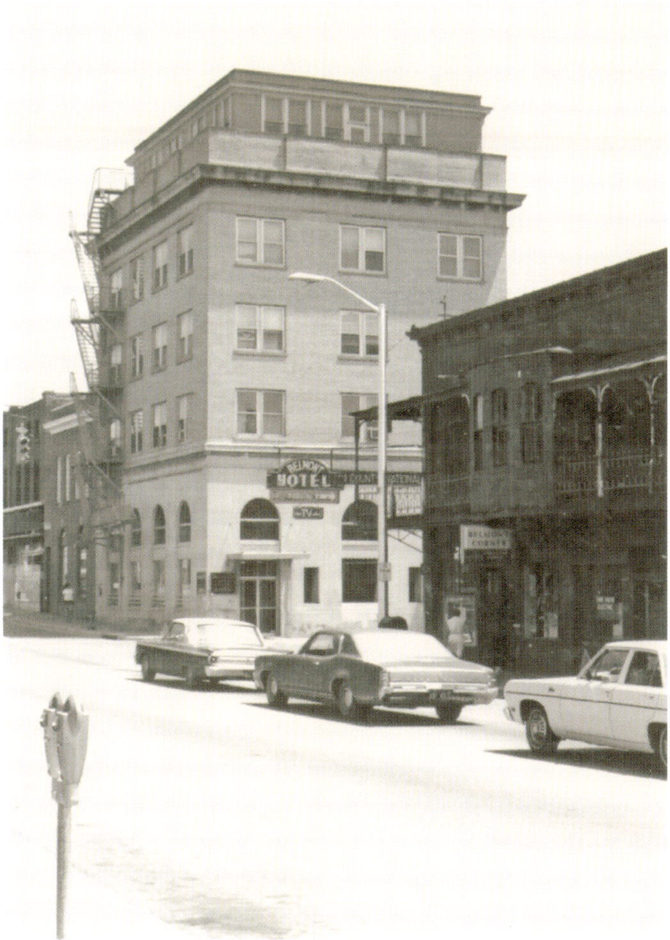

People's National Bank. Standing on the corner of Wall and Main Streets, this handsome brick building was built in 1923 with four stories, the first in Abingdon. A frame fifth floor was even added on top in 1924 as a meeting space. The bank failed during the Depression, and in 1934, Washington County National Bank opened here. It has been occupied by different banks since that time. The building has been renovated and added on to through the years. (Peggy Johnson.)

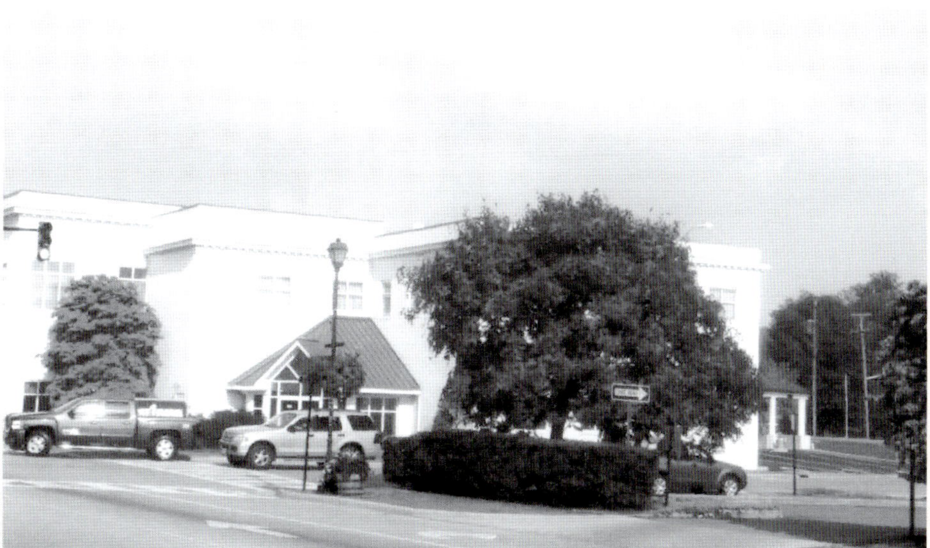

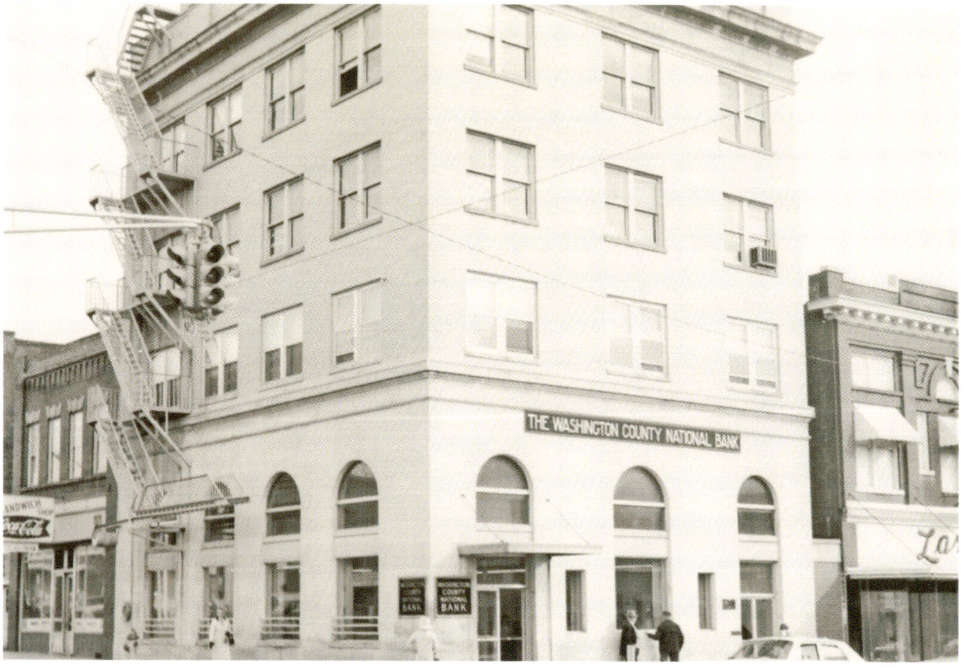

People's National Bank, 1966. This large building has been home to several banks, including the People's National Bank, the Washington County National Bank (in the vintage photograph above), and Central Fidelity Bank. The exterior fire escape was a prominent fixture on the Main Street side. Though it was the first four-story building in town, the upper floors were removed, and today it only boasts two stories. (Peggy Johnson.)

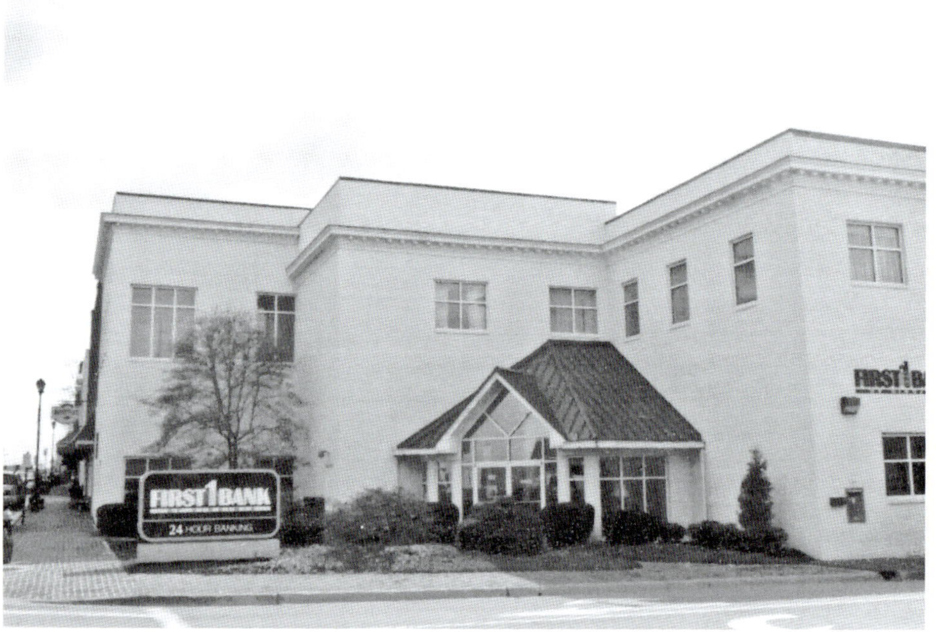

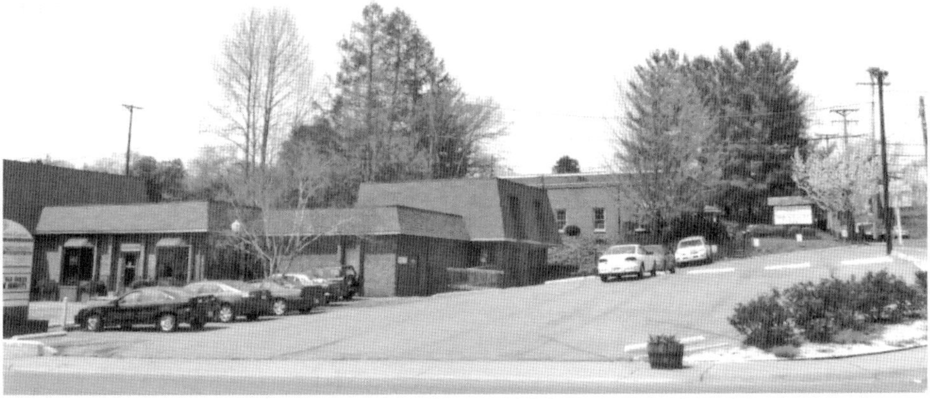

BP Service Station. For many years, this BP service station was a busy downtown destination and gathering spot. The building was located at the corner of Russell Road and Main Street, as shown in the 1971 photograph below. The station was torn down and new office buildings erected on the lot after 1980. (Peggy Johnson.)

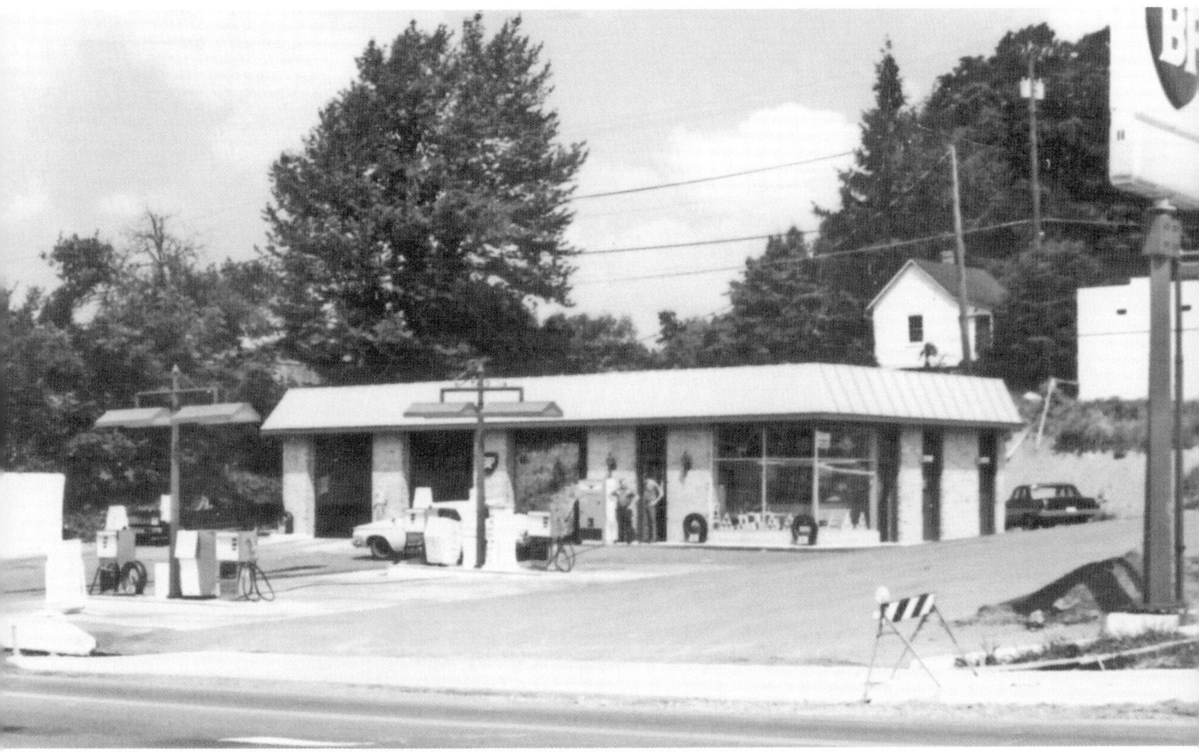

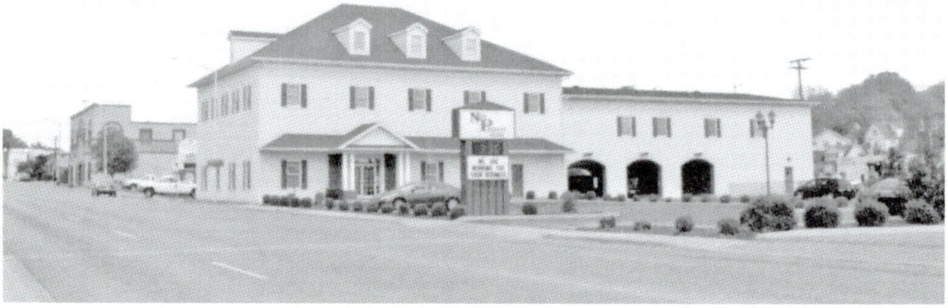

Texaco Gas. Owned by Sam Repass, this gas station served downtown customers for years. Radio Shack occupied the adjacent building, which today is used for a bank. The Texaco was demolished, and the space is the parking lot for the adjacent bank today. (Courtesy Lynda Campbell.)

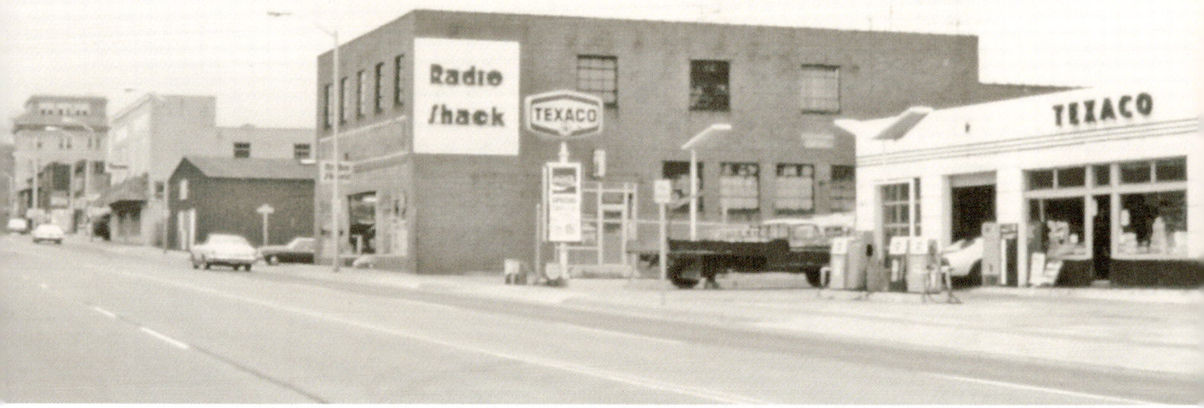

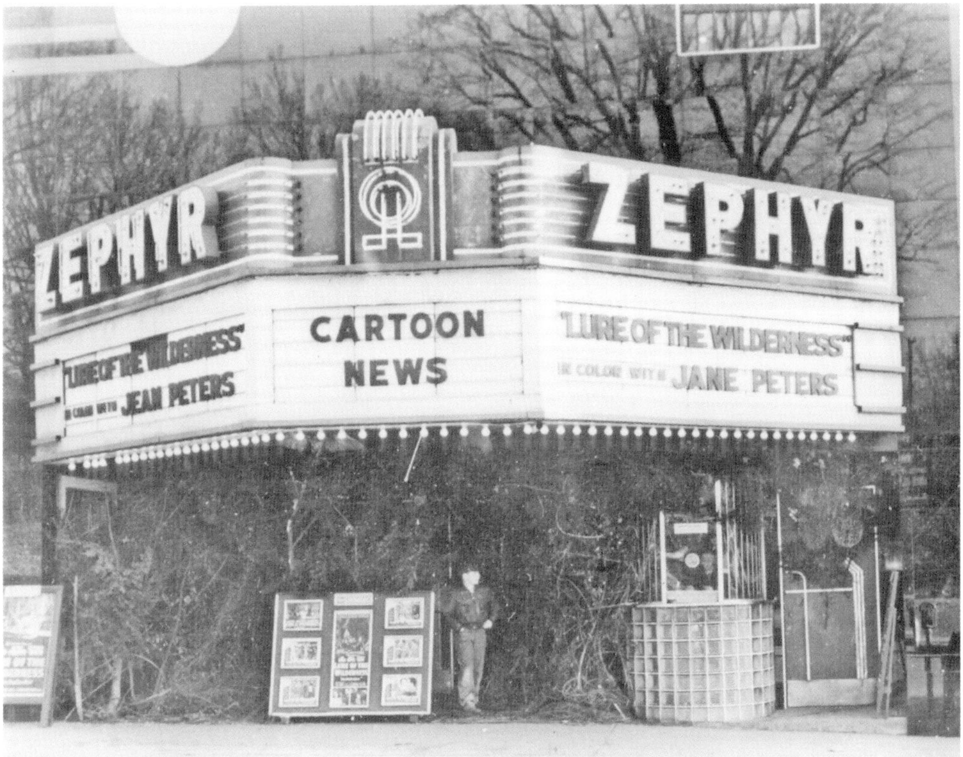

Zephyr Theatre. Downtown's popular Zephyr Theatre was showing *Lure of the Wilderness* in color with Jane Peters in 1952. Operated by Lincoln Theatres Corporation of Marion, Virginia, the Zephyr was Abingdon's best—the first modern theater in the area. Seeing a movie at the Zephyr was a popular pastime until it closed about 1963. The building has been occupied by commercial shops since that time. (Doug Patterson, Allen Gregory.)

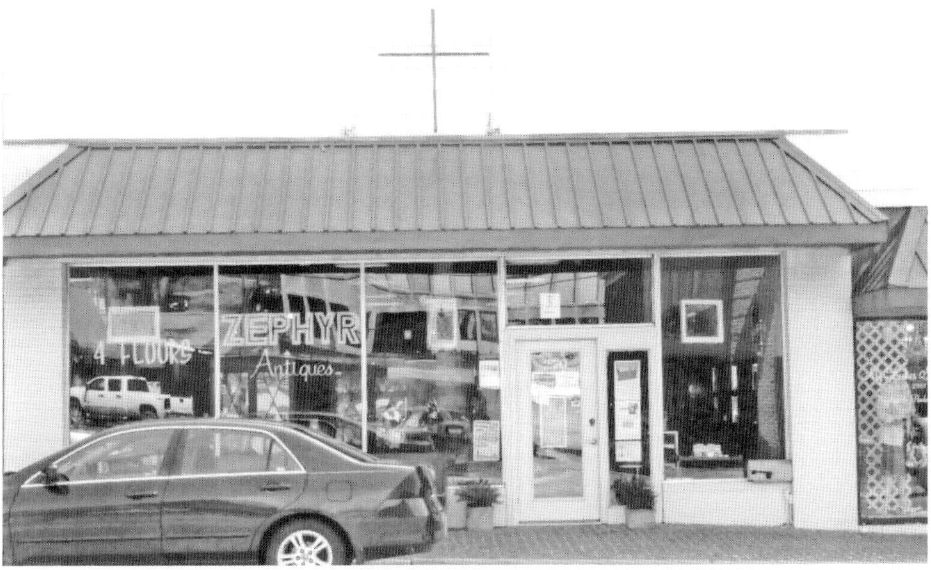

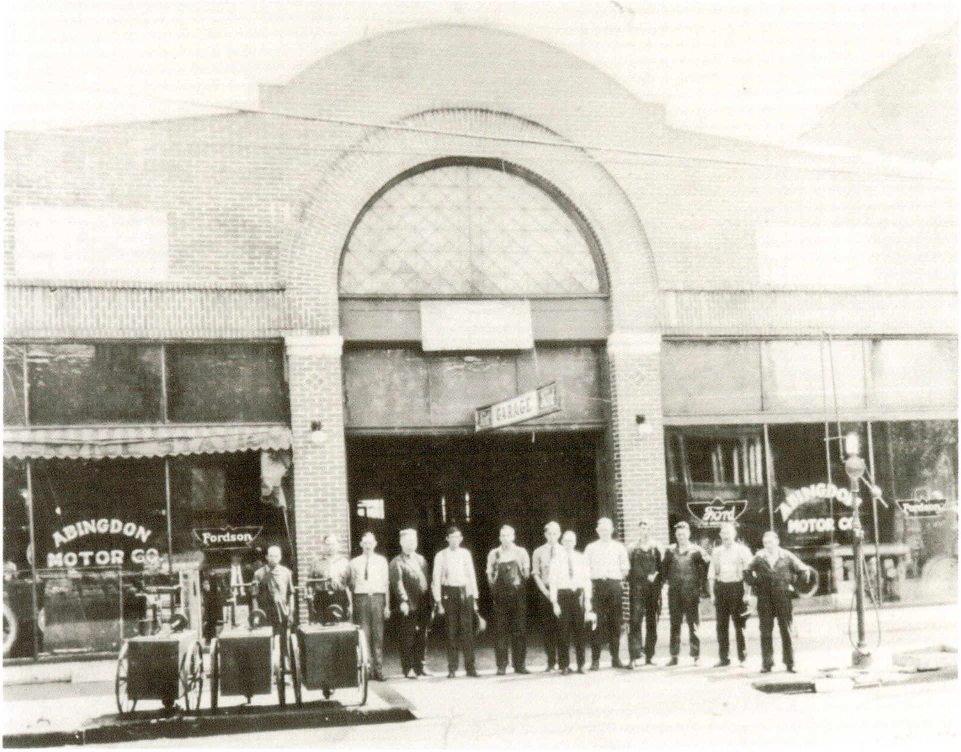

ABINGDON MOTOR COMPANY, 1920. William and J. T. McConnell built this large auto repair shop and garage in 1919, and it was later purchased by J. F. Drugan with Abingdon Motor Company. The building retained this use until 1949, when Appalachian Power Company located there. Pictured above from left to right are unidentified, Lewis Arnett, Jim Graham, Sunshine Summer, James R. Harris, Glen McCall, three unidentified, Charles W. Harris, Bruce Phelps, unidentified, and Ralph Ward. (Lorena Harris Bolling and Margaret Harris.)

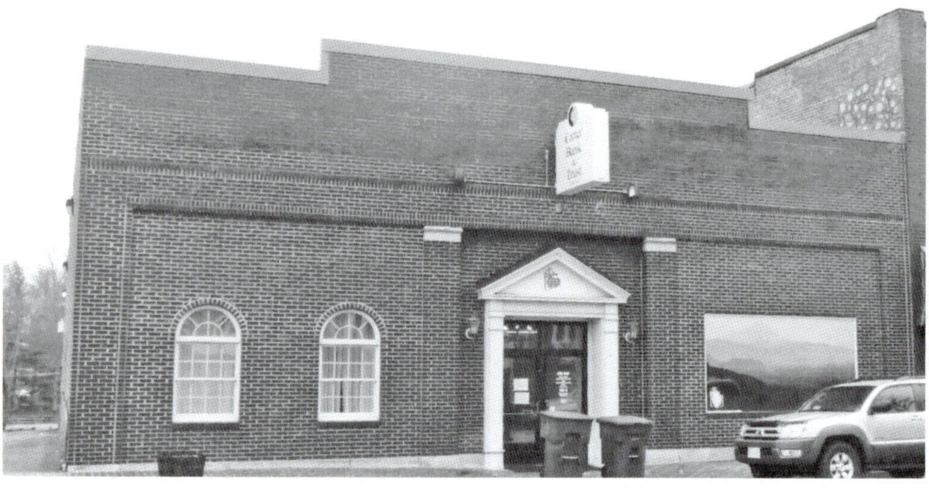

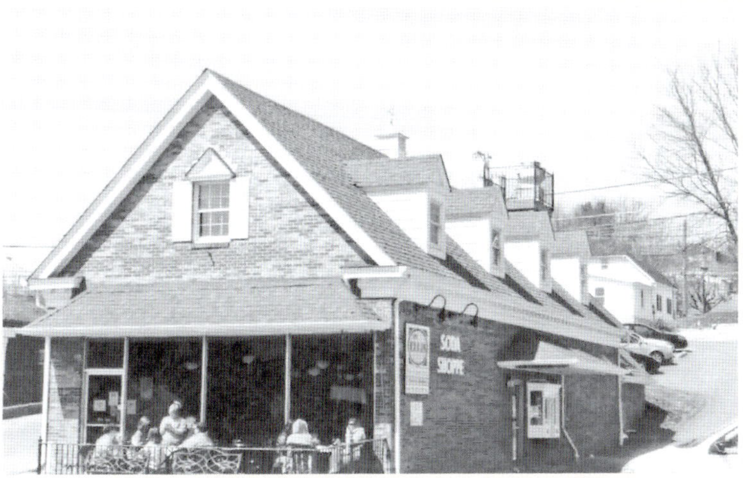

Ellis Pharmacy, 1975. Founded by Harold R. Ellis, the locals' favorite, Ellis Pharmacy, had been located in the old Farmers Exchange Bank building, but in 1959, "Pop" Ellis constructed this building. Lovely oak and glass cabinetry from the old Abingdon Pharmacy was saved and installed inside. No longer a pharmacy, the building now hosts a restaurant owned by the Ellis family that has become a local favorite as well. (Then, Town of Abingdon; now, Norma Meade.)

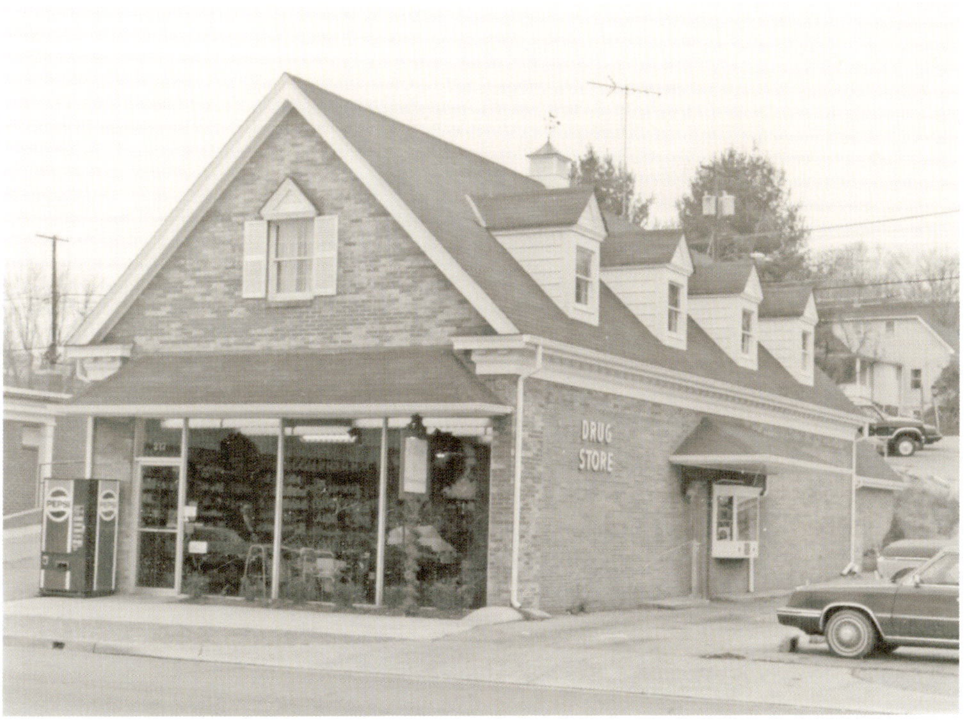

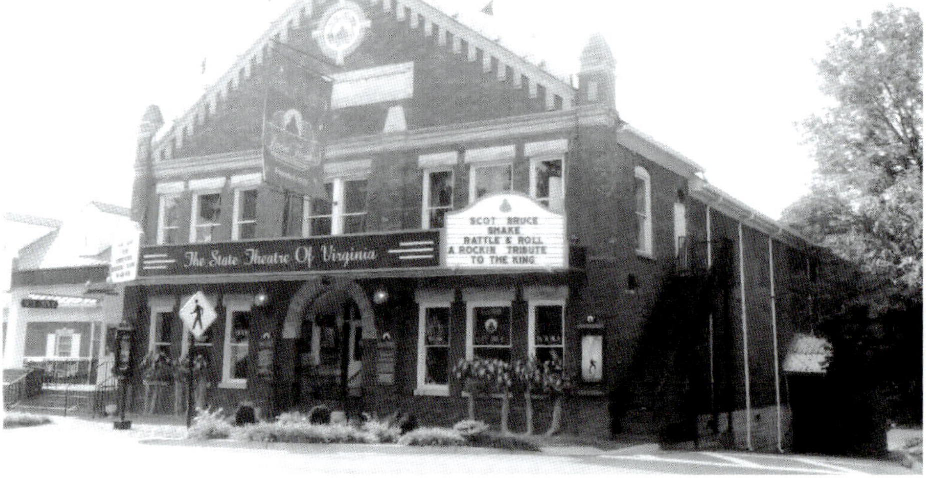

Barter Theatre in 1966. The Barter Theatre's central section was built for the Sinking Spring Presbyterian Church around 1832, but later uses included a temperance hall and town hall. Founded in 1933 by Robert Porterfield, the theater provided hungry actors with food from farmers hungry for entertainment. The barter system continued for many years, but today one must purchase a ticket to see a play. The Rodefer house (1856) is visible to the east of the theater. (Then, Peggy Johnson; now, Norma Meade.)

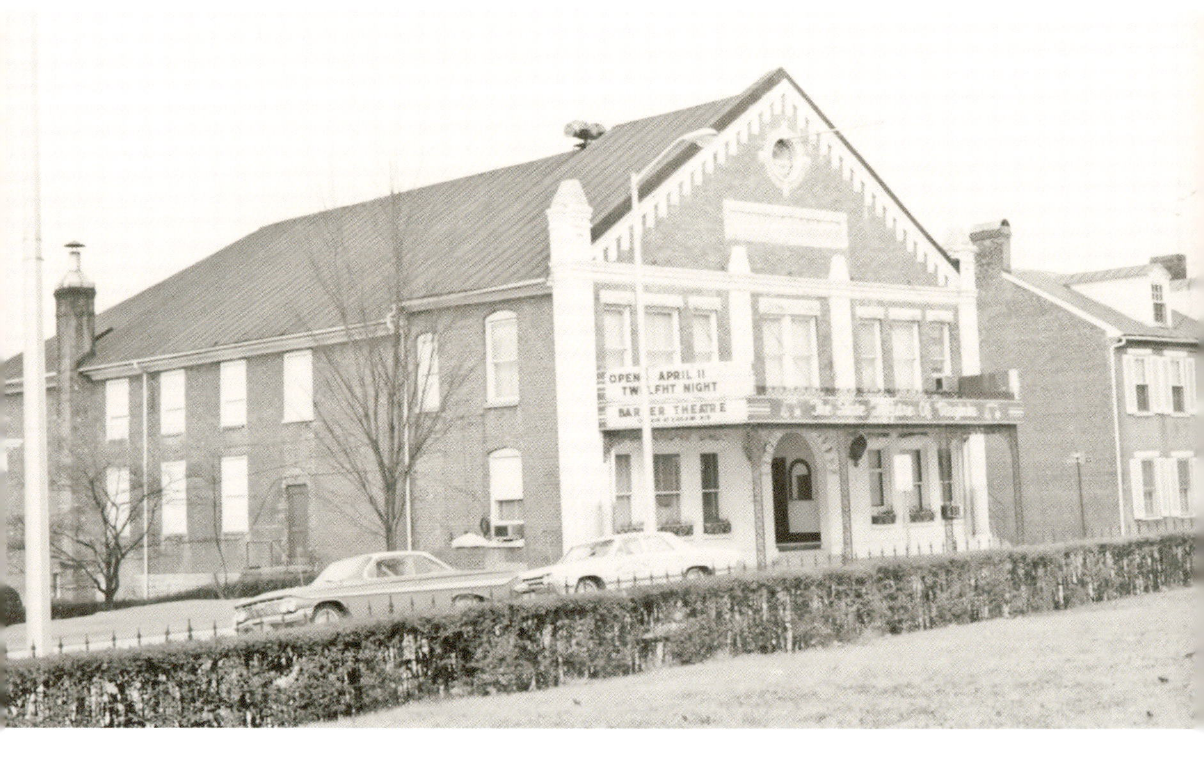

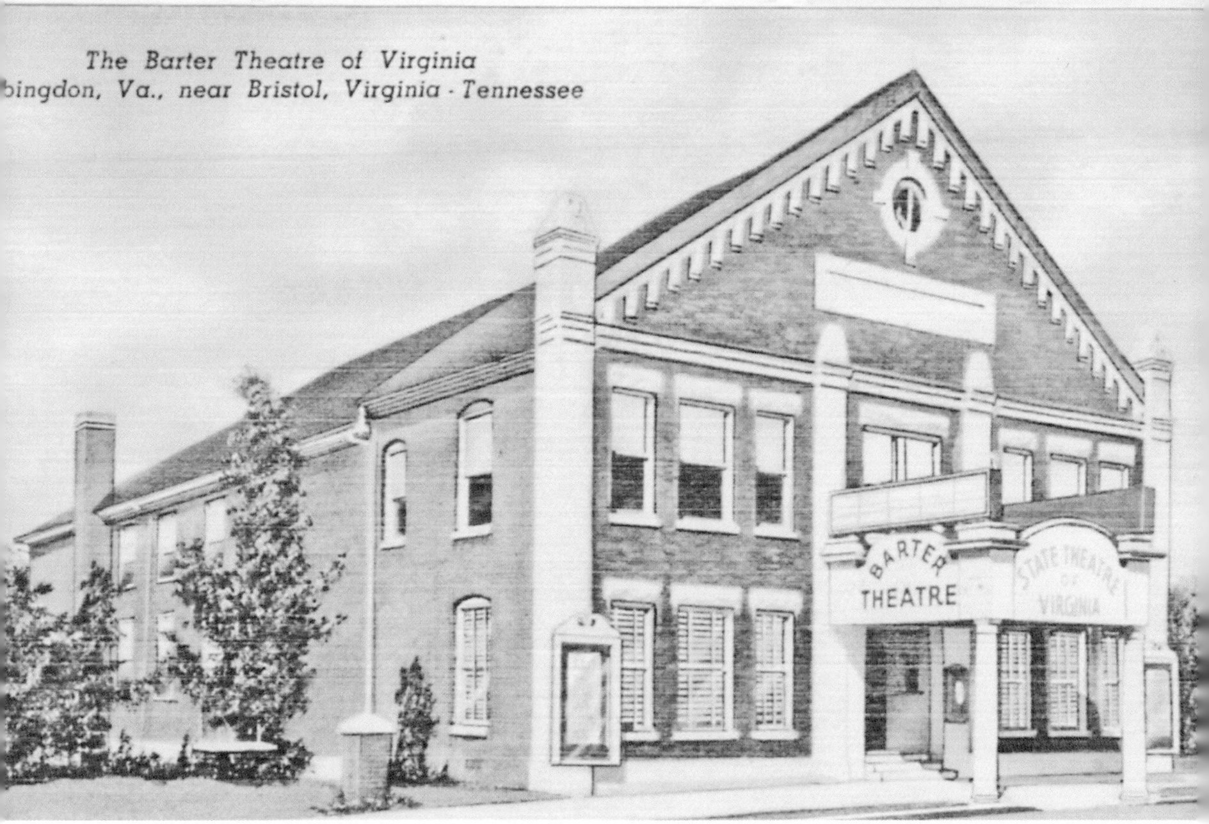

BARTER THEATRE, VIRGINIA'S STATE THEATRE. As the vintage postcard portrays, the Barter Theatre became a popular destination with locals and visitors. Many folks still plan a trip to Abingdon just to attend a play at the Barter Theatre. The postcard above predated the addition on the west side that expanded the seating space. Although Gothic details have been added, the building has retained its historic character. (Myra Worsham Martin.)

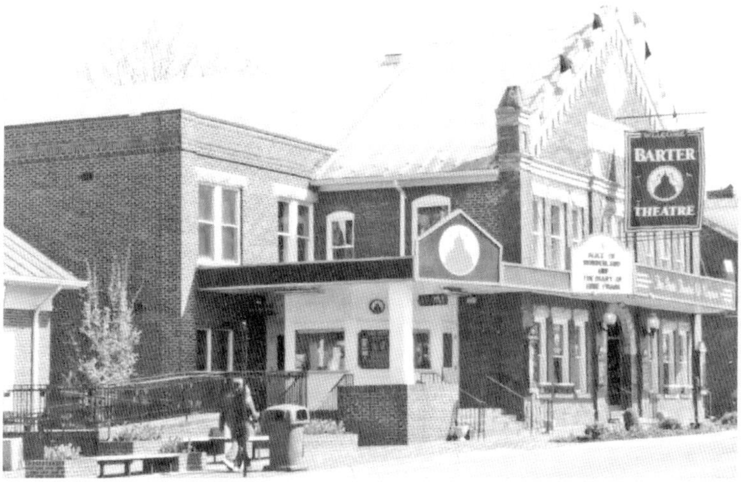

***John Loves Mary* at the Barter Theatre.** The theater proudly advertised the latest show: "Tonite *John Loves Mary* latest Broadway smash by Norman Krasna." The theater was key in bringing culture to this rural town and important in setting it apart from other towns in the region. Still popular today, the theater performs off-Broadway plays and musicals and draws visitors from all over the United States. (Myra Worsham Martin.)

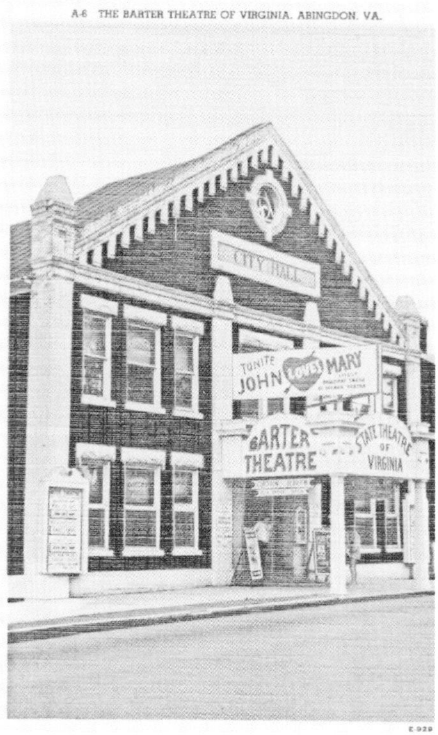

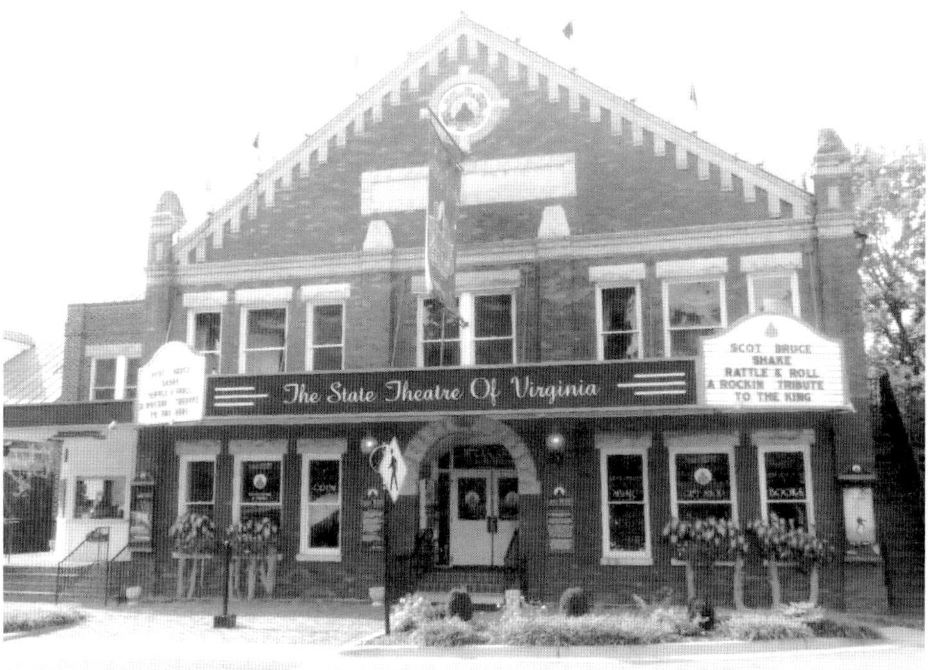

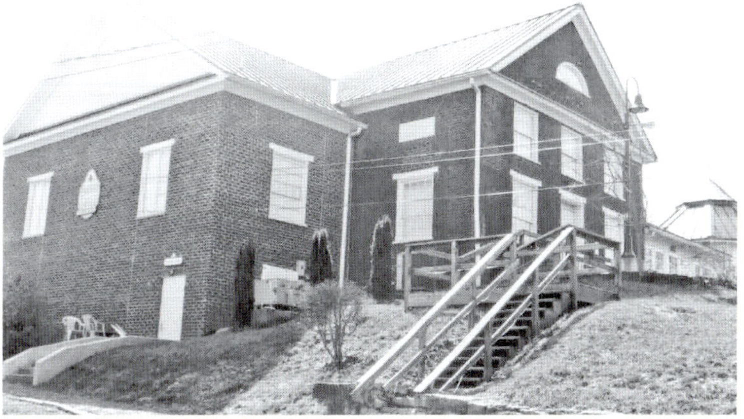

METHODIST CHURCH/BARTER PLAYHOUSE. This Greek Revival–style building was built in 1831 for the Methodist Protestant church, which separated from the Methodist Episcopal church. The building has been owned by the Barter Theatre for many years and is known as the Barter Stage II, providing a smaller, more intimate stage. The building underwent renovations several years ago, and additions were made to the building. (Town of Abingdon and Norma Meade.)

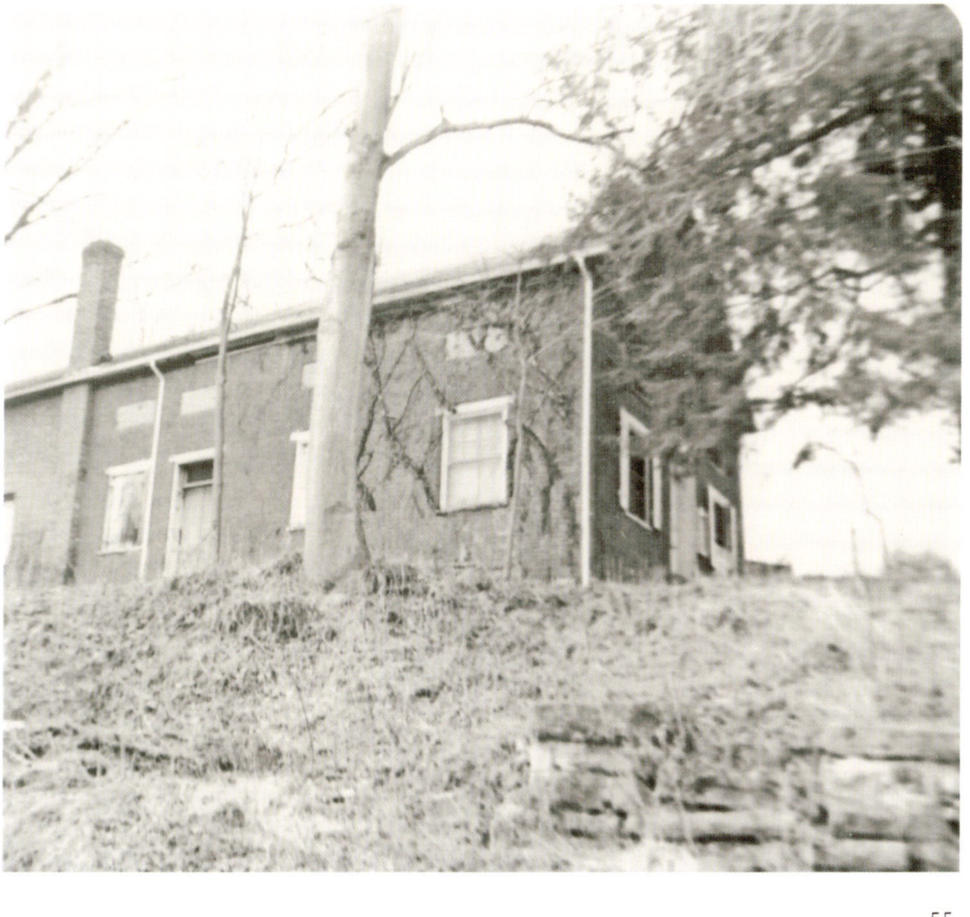

KELLER STOREHOUSE. This narrow two-story brick building was built for commercial use in 1883 by Samuel G. Keller, a local merchant. A grocery store used the first floor, and G. N. Wertz operated a busy photography studio on the second floor. Previous to this building, the lot contained a log structure used for a hat manufactory. Different commercial enterprises have been located in the building over time, and the building has been well maintained. (Town of Abingdon.)

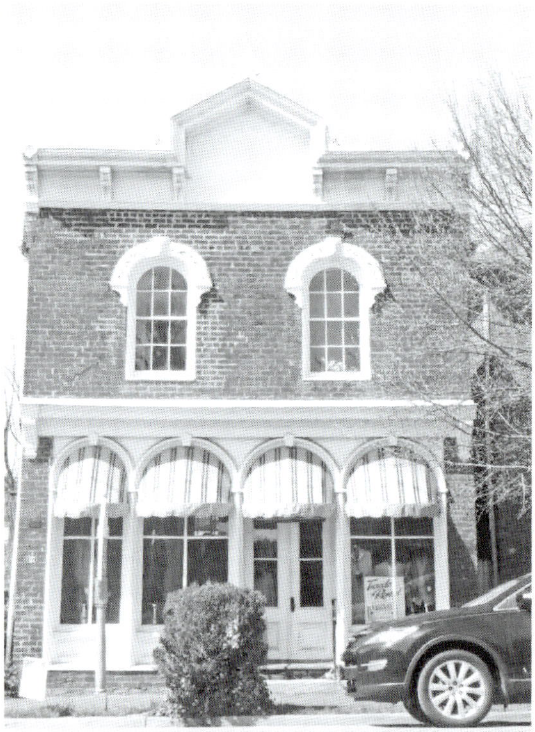

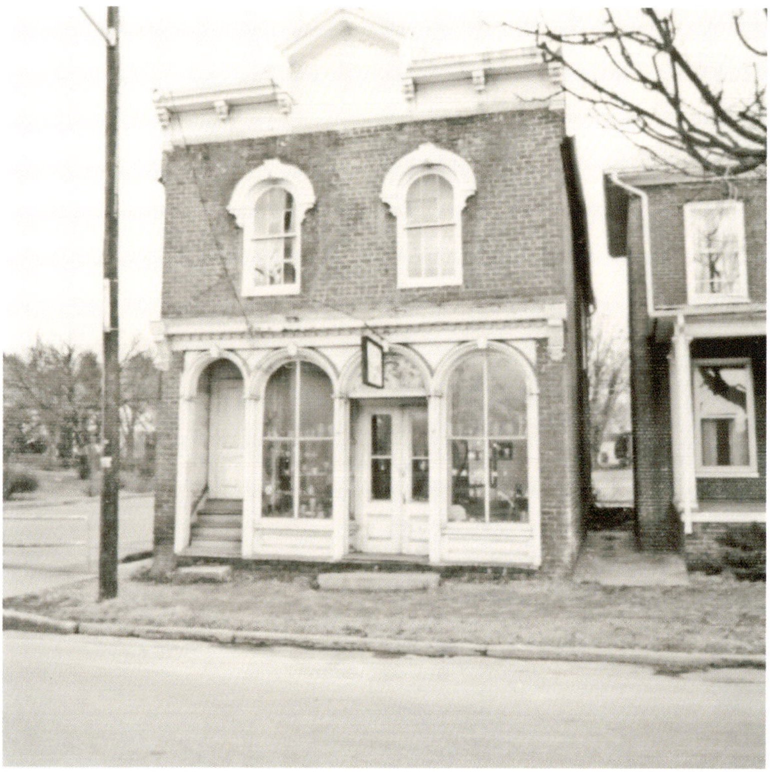

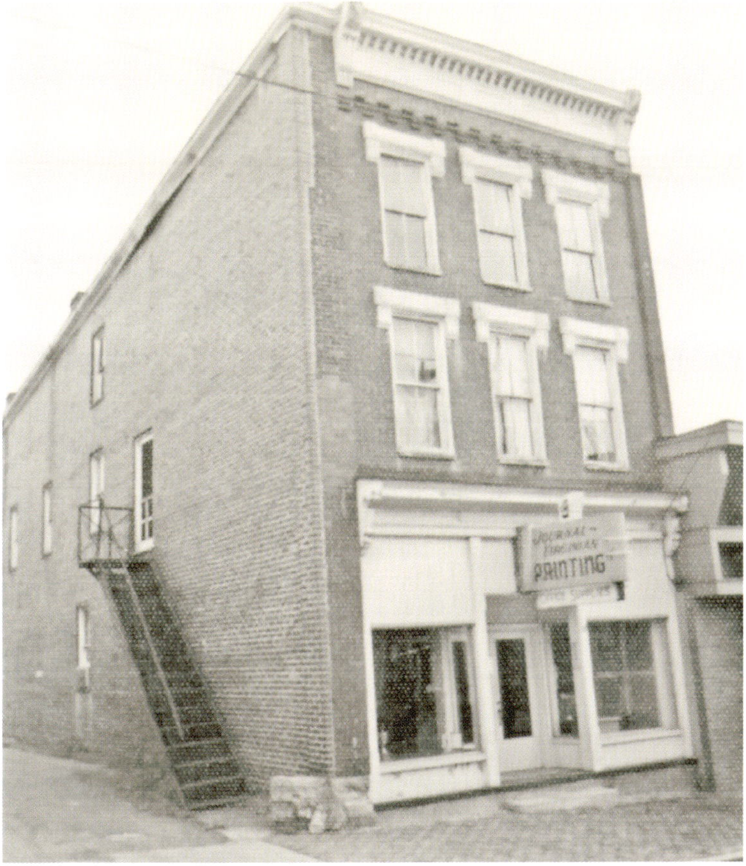

Minter Jackson Store. This three-story brick building was constructed in 1886 by Minter Jackson and was occupied by Washington Hardware, the Abingdon Dispensary, and various local newspapers. The *Abingdon-Virginian*, a popular and outspoken local newspaper, operated from this building for more than 70 years. The building is currently used as a museum and residence. (Town of Abingdon.)

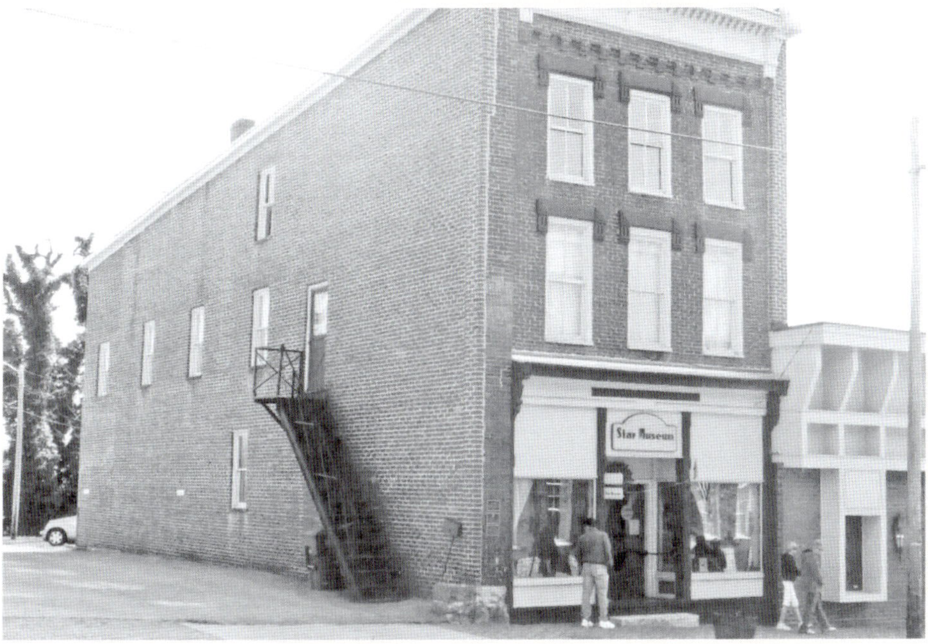

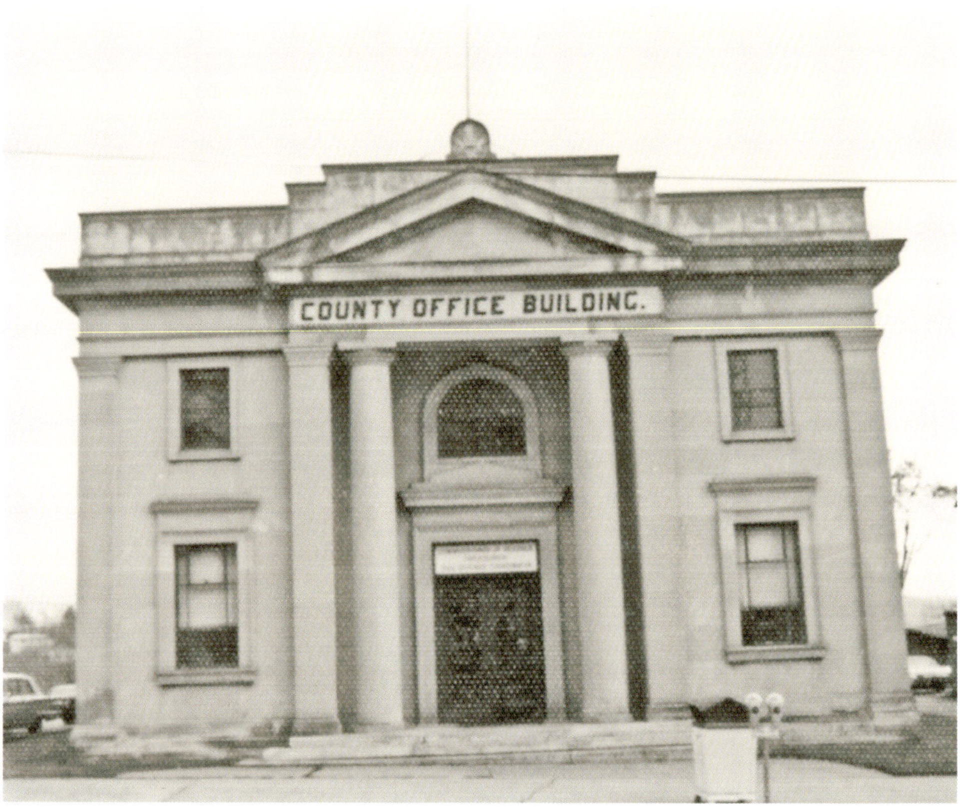

First National Bank of Abingdon. Designed by Clarence Kearfott of Bristol, this imposing building was constructed in 1923 for the First National Bank of Abingdon, with luxurious details such as marble floors and mahogany woodwork. Washington County purchased the building in 1938, when the bank was liquidated, and today, the building houses county offices. (Town of Abingdon.)

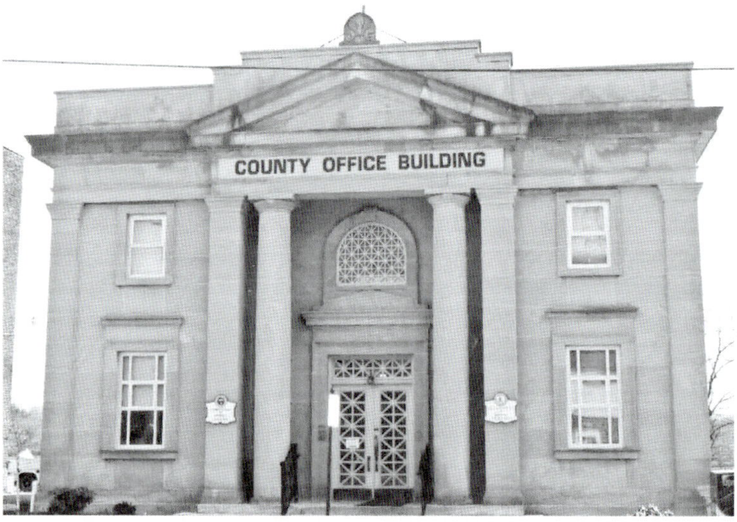

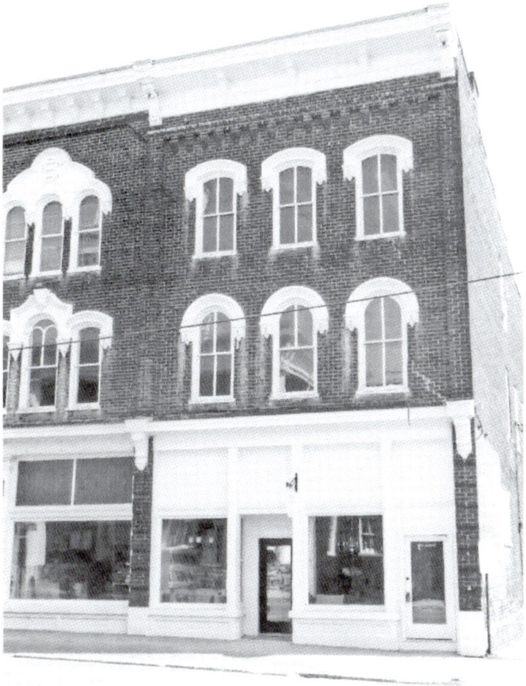

GREENWAY BROTHERS BUILDING. As the initials carved above the center window state, these buildings were constructed in 1878 by James C. Greenway, David C. Greenway, and Thomas Preston Trigg. They were constructed as a three-part building and housed a banking room and vault, stores, offices, and storage; later a grocery store and the Abingdon Pharmacy occupied the east side. The *c.* 1973 and modern photographs show that the buildings still retain their historic character. (Town of Abingdon.)

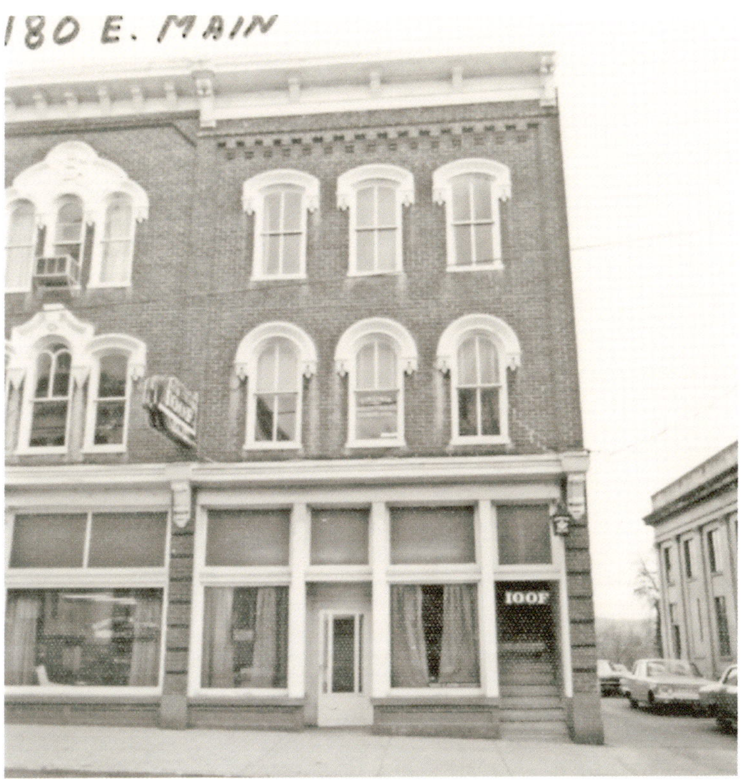

The Corner Restaurant, 1972. Lewis P. Summers changed the facade of this eastern third of the Greenway Brothers Building (1878) to match the Dagmar building on the east side. The Corner restaurant operated from the building for many years and was a popular lunchroom and soda fountain from the 1930s through the 1960s. Attorneys' offices were located on the second floor, and the space continues to be used as offices today. (Town of Abingdon.)

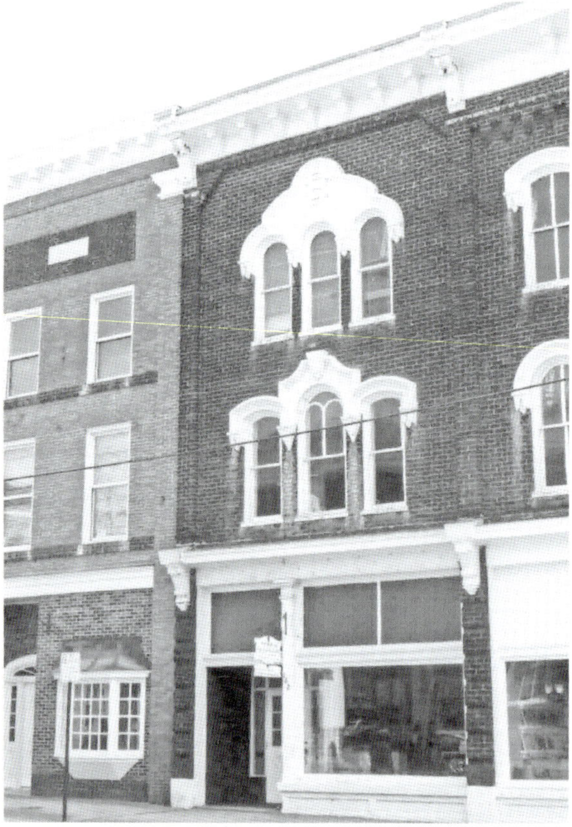

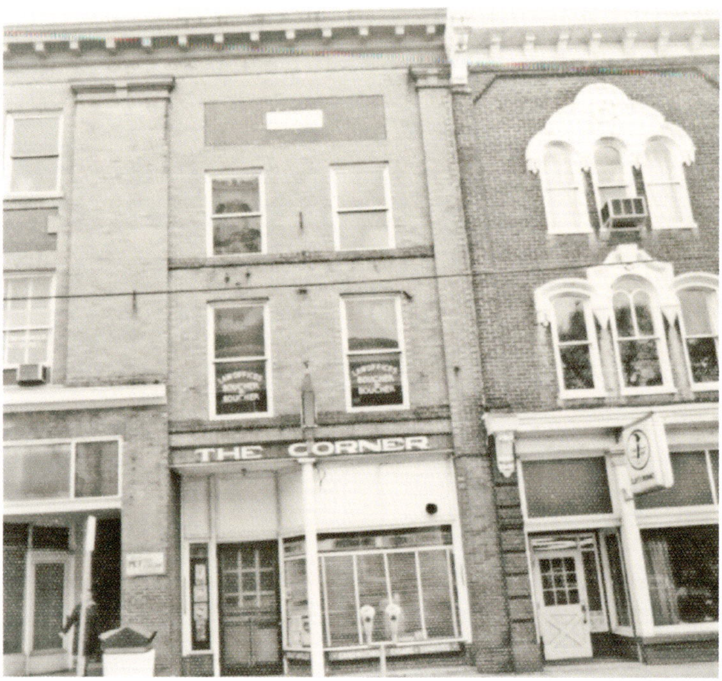

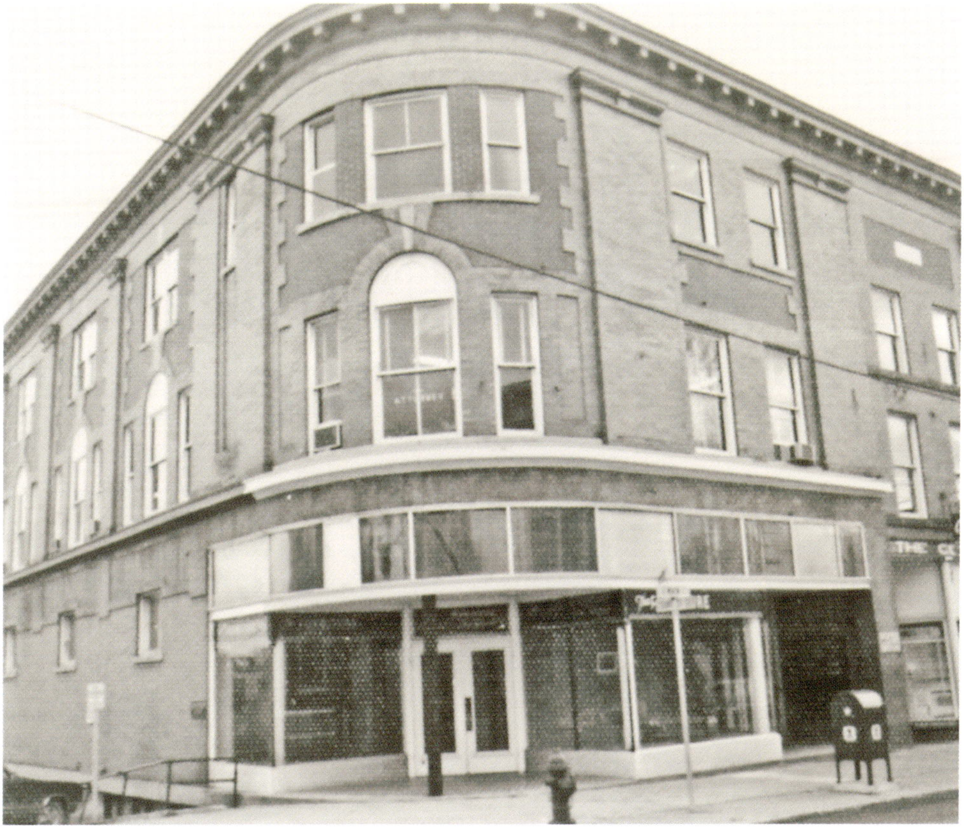

Dagmar Hotel. Lewis P. Summers constructed this curved building in 1911 and established the Dagmar Hotel, complete with barbershop, billiard hall, dining room, and lodging rooms. The building temporarily housed the Stonewall Jackson College after it burned in 1914. In 1919, the building was used for a furniture store and undertaking business. Today, the building is used for the offices of Congressman Rick Boucher, with attorneys' offices upstairs. (Then, Town of Abingdon; now, Norma Meade.)

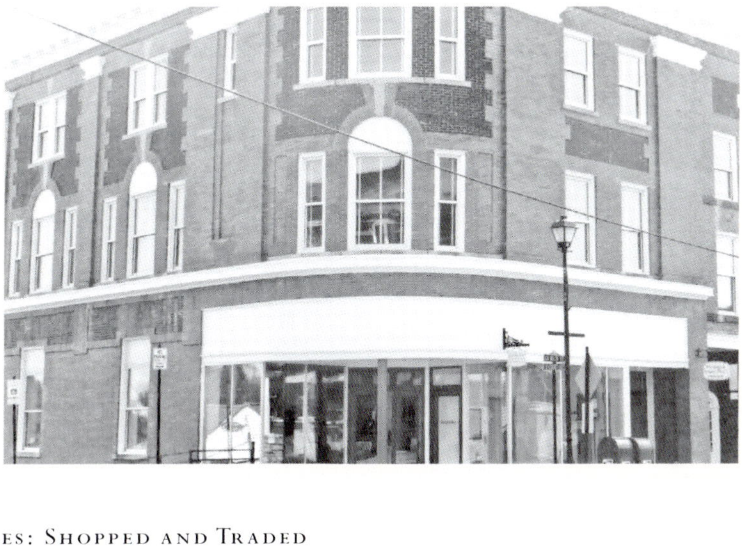

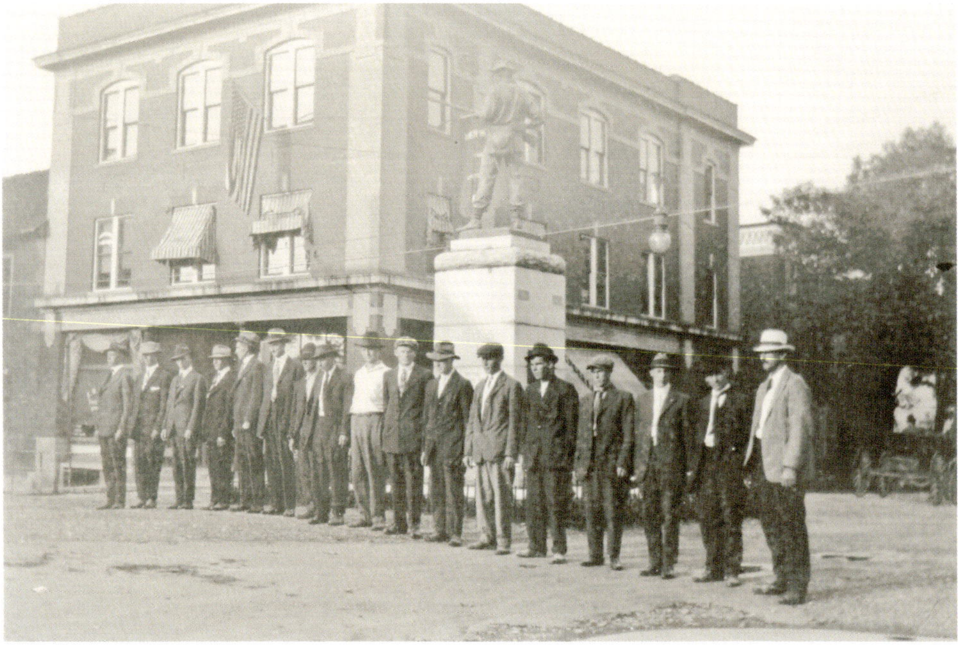

Summers Building and Confederate Statue. This group of dapper gentlemen seems to be lined up for a special occasion across Main Street in front of the Confederate soldier statue and the Summers building (1908). This lot has been home to a pre-1786 house and William King's brick house (1803), the first such house in town. The *c.* 1940 photograph predates when the statue was moved to the side yard of the courthouse due to auto traffic. (Historical Society of Washington County.)

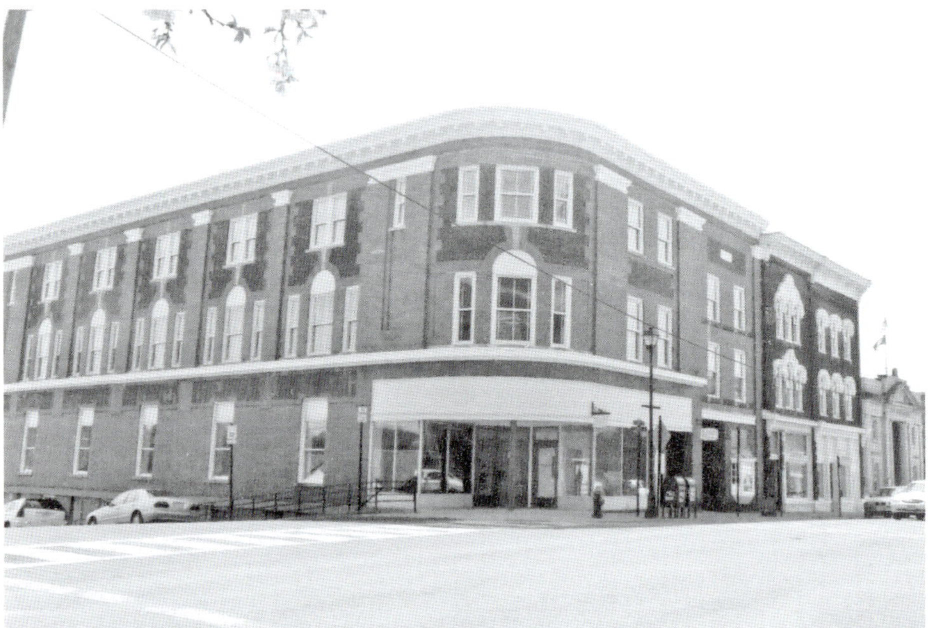

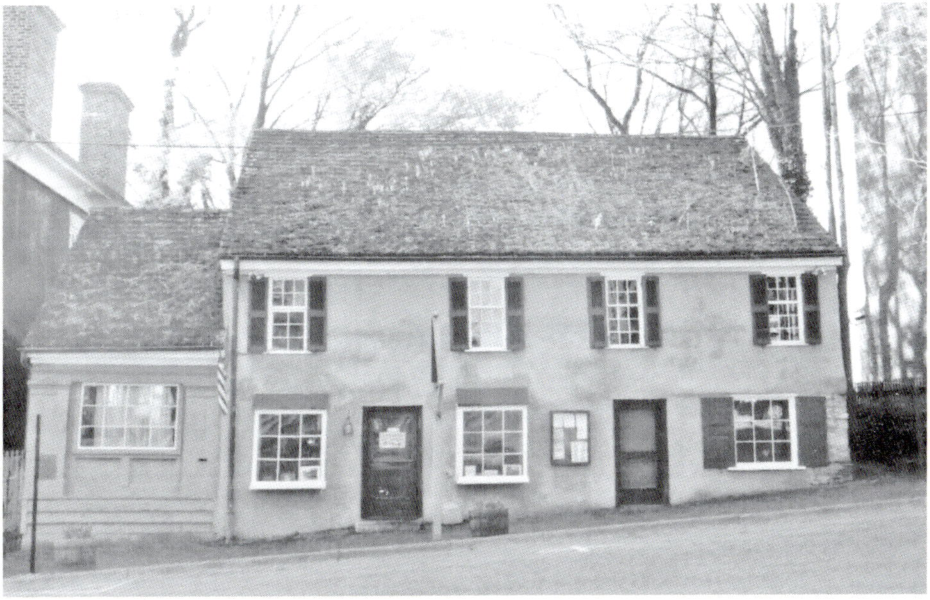

The Tavern, 1940. Although historically several taverns were located in town, today only one remains in business, and it is believed to have been built around 1788. With uses through the years including a tavern, residence, bank, bakery, general store, barbershop, post office, and retail store, this building has become a regional destination. Nowadays, this unique stucco-and-stone building is used for an upscale restaurant. (Historical Society of Washington County.)

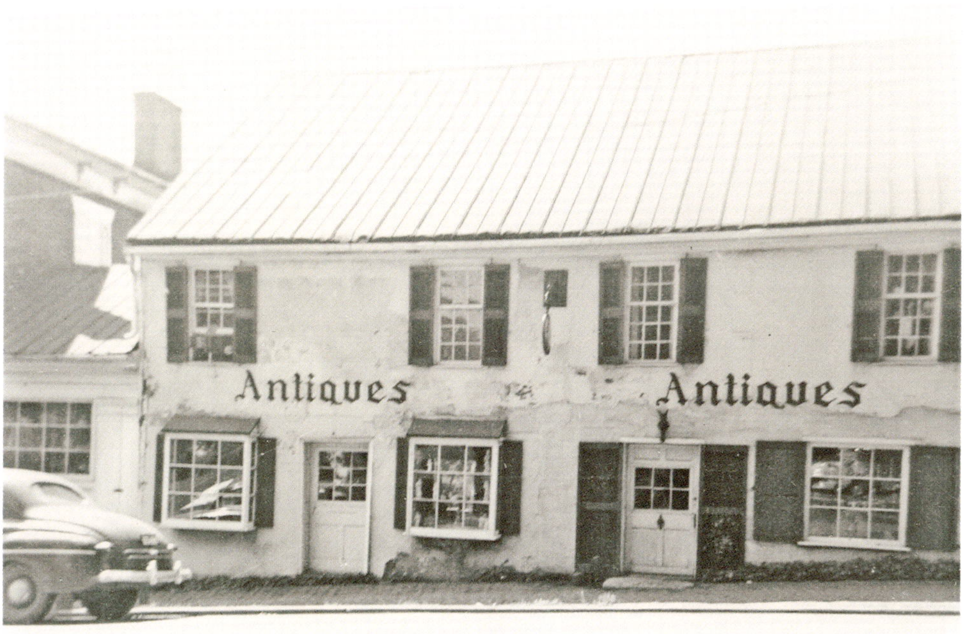

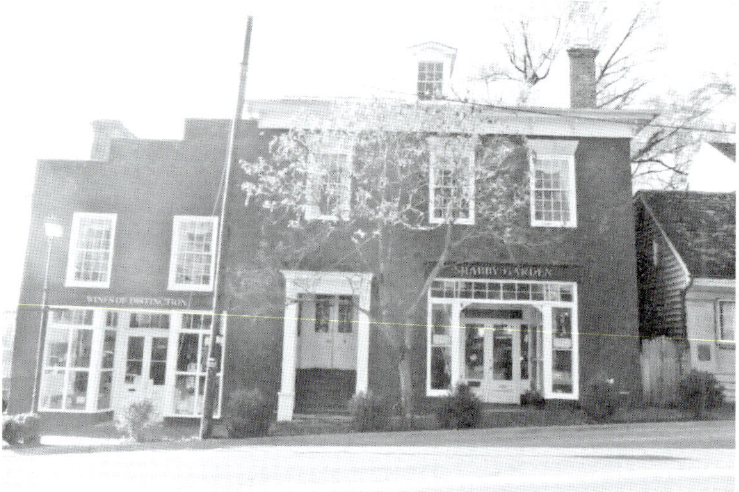

WASHINGTON HOUSE/THOMAS FINDLAY HOTEL. Several earlier buildings, including a log tavern, a residence, a lumber house, and an ordinary (providing meals and lodging) owned by a freed slave named Fincastle Sterrett, occupied this lot. Shown below around 1930, the Washington House, Abingdon's first hotel, was built by Thomas Findlay in 1835. Later used as a boardinghouse, Clark Brothers Meat Market, and a millinery shop, this building today is used for retail purposes. (Historical Society of Washington County.)

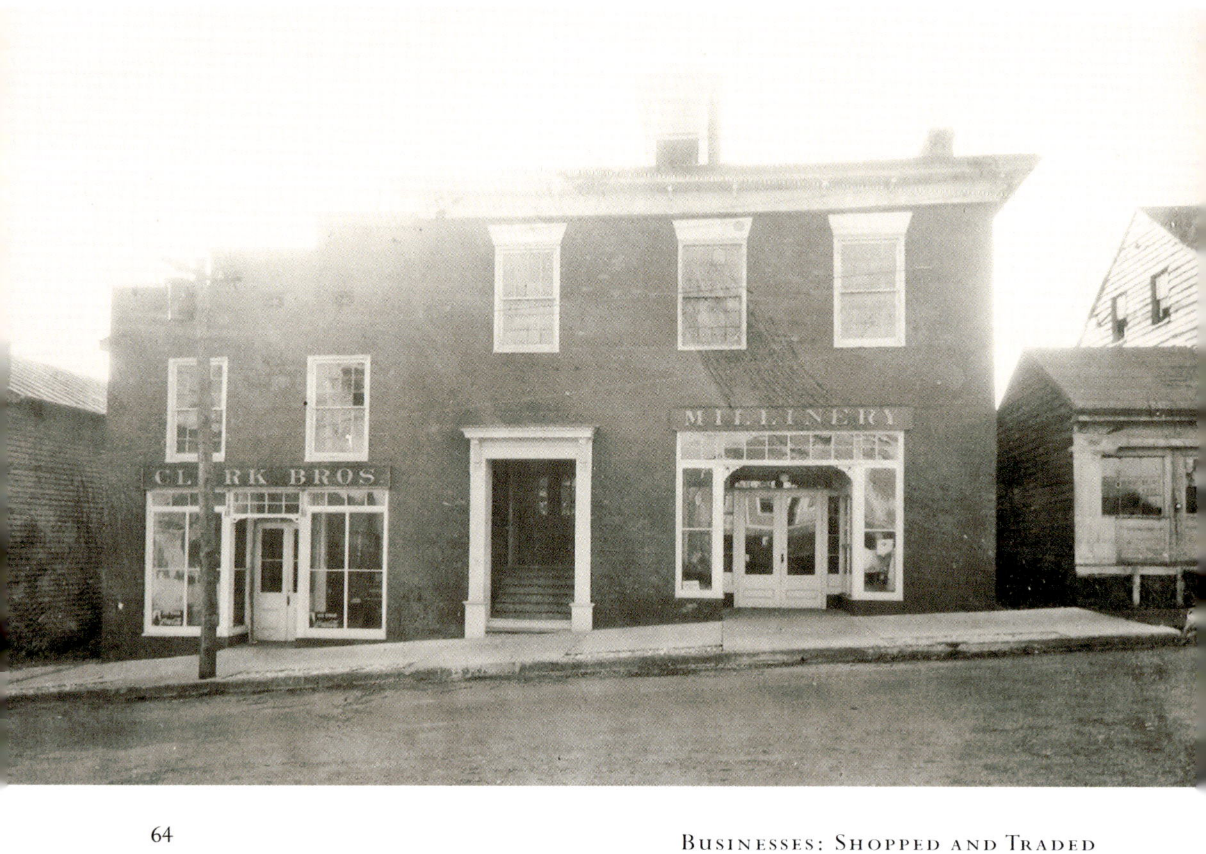

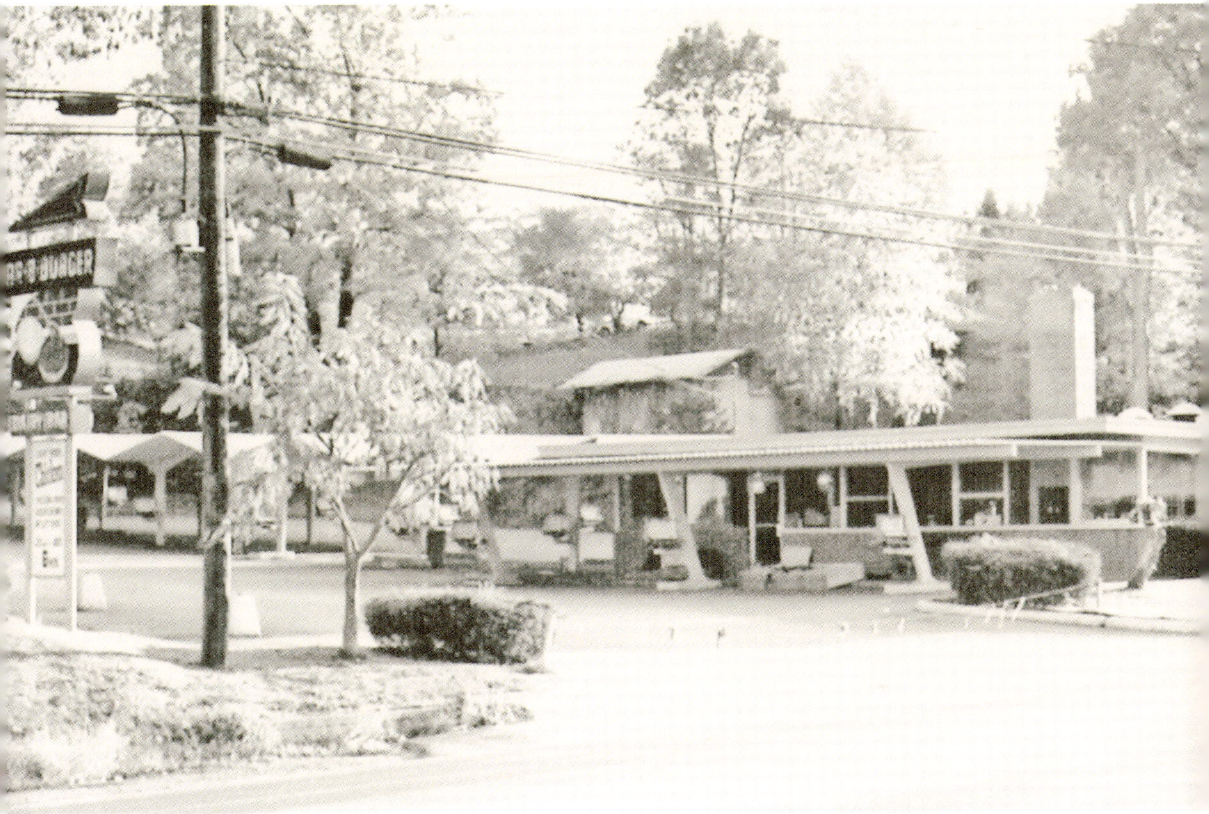

Bar-B-Burger Drive-In. Shown above around 1965, the Bar-B-Burger Drive-in was an institution on the western end of Main Street and provided friendly curb service and the best burgers in town. It was owned by Frank Widener and later became the Fireside Restaurant. Today it is Alison's Restaurant, still a location for delicious food but now with indoor seating. (Lynda Campbell.)

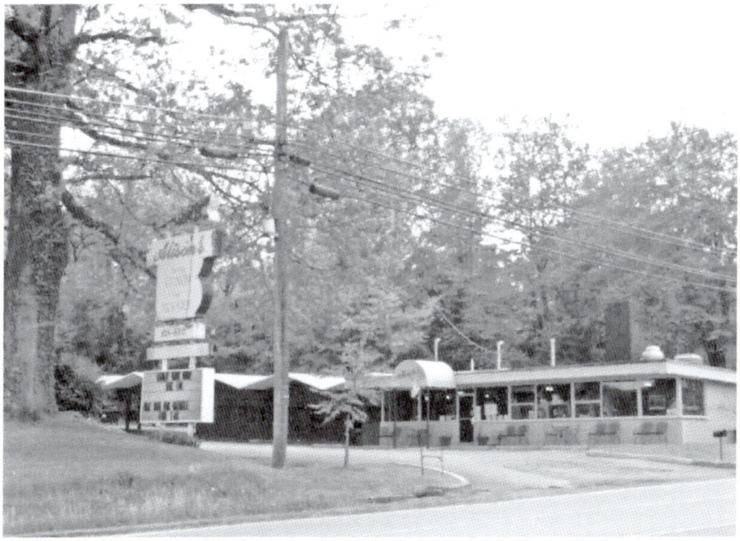

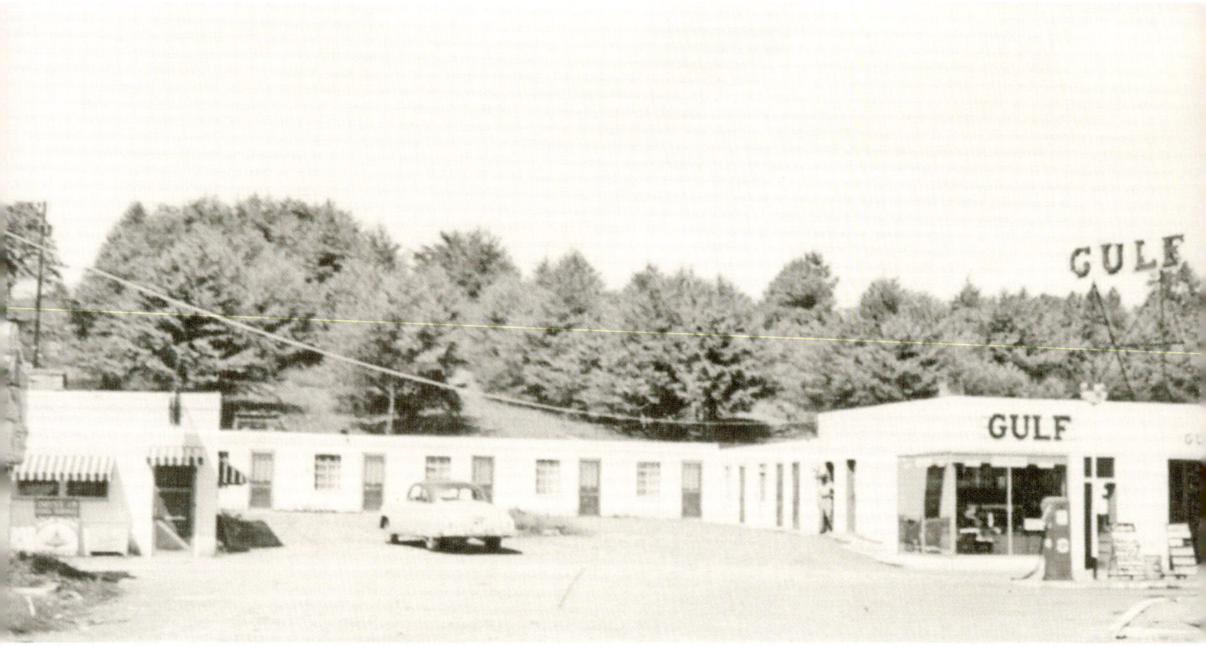

Taylor's Motel and Gulf Station. Taylor's Motel and the Gulf station were once located at the western edge of Main Street. The hotel advertised "9 modern units, radiant heat, modern showers, restaurant serving fine foods only" and was owned and operated by Walter and R. F. (Bob) Taylor. Today, the motel section is used for storage, and the station building is an auto parts store and service center. (Janice Taylor Duncan.)

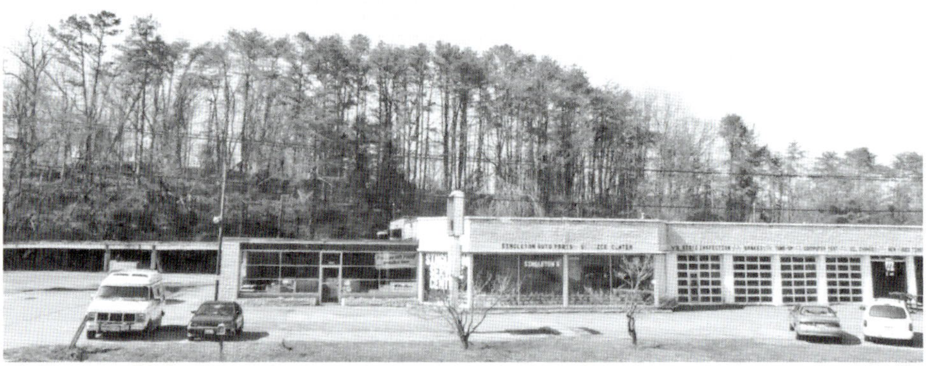

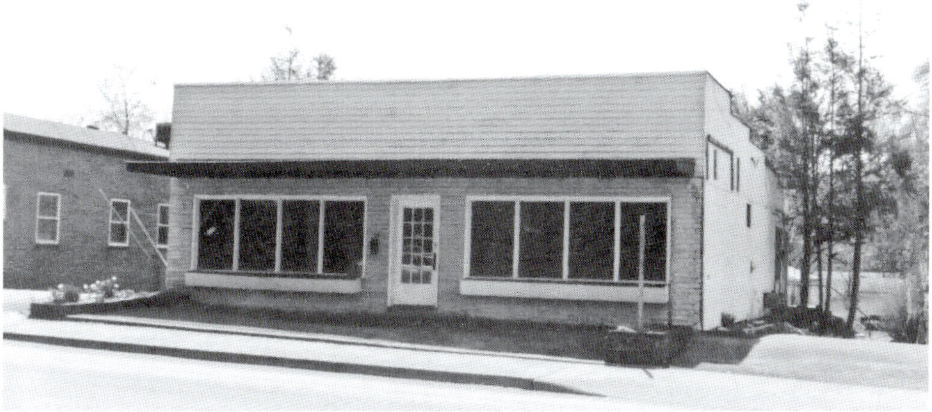

Cumbow China. Still collectible, Cumbow China was decorated by local artisans for years in the buildings adjacent to their retail store, shown here. Founded in 1921 by Mabel Cumbow and Jacob Zachariah Ruskin, Cumbow Lustreware was so popular that it was sent as a gift to King George VI and Queen Elizabeth of England, as well as Pres. Franklin D. and Eleanor Roosevelt. After Mabel's death in 1980, the business was discontinued. Today, this building is occupied by retail stores. (Peggy Johnson.)

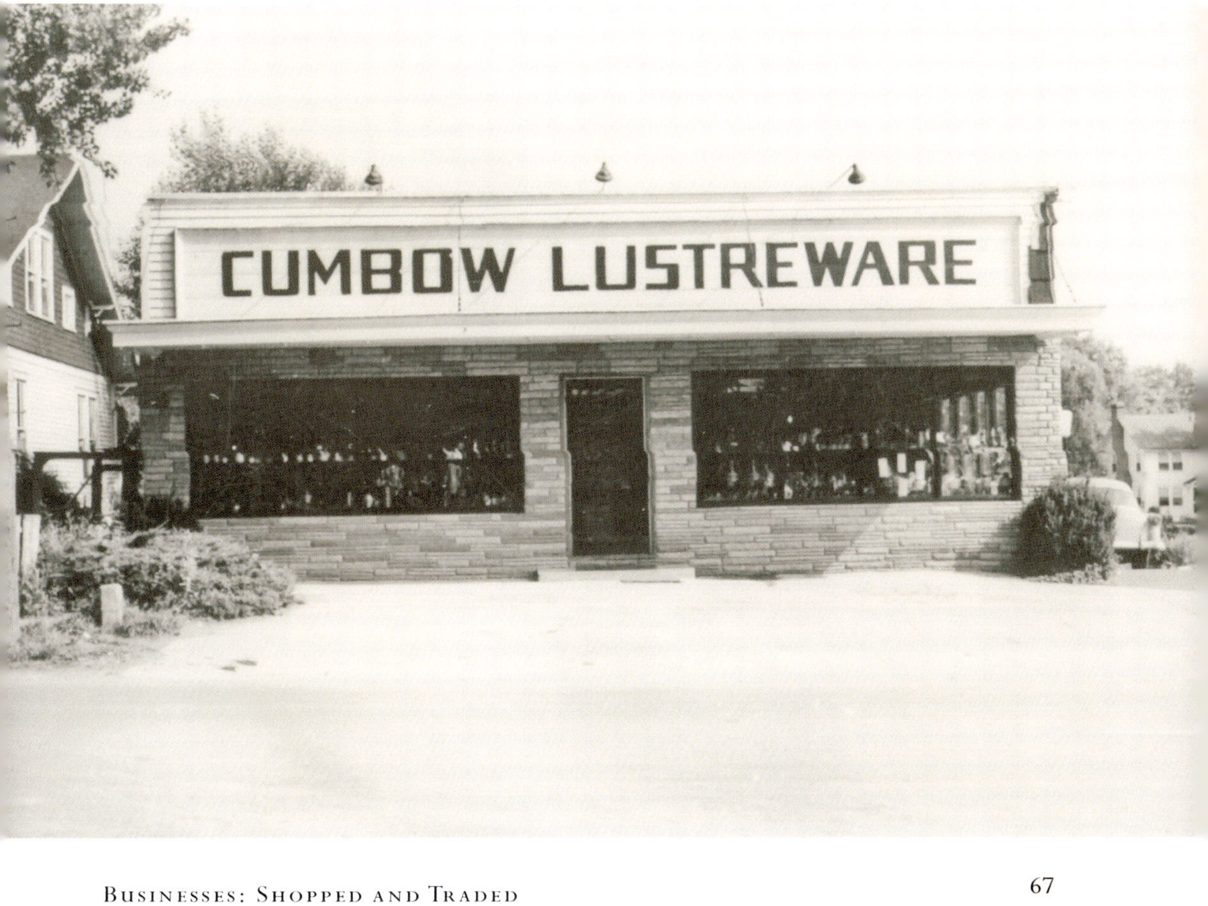

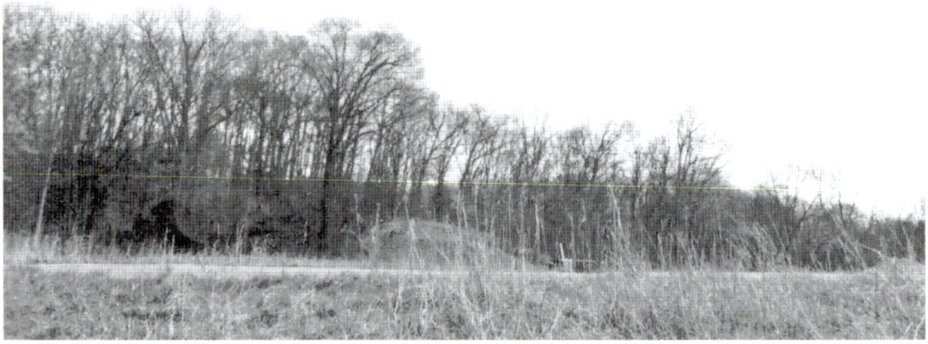

Glenrochie Club House. The first clubhouse for the Glenrochie Country Club was built in 1958, shown in the early photograph below. It was demolished in 2000 after the new, larger clubhouse was developed and built just below it. Today's lovely brick clubhouse hosts group events and a restaurant. (Ben Abel.)

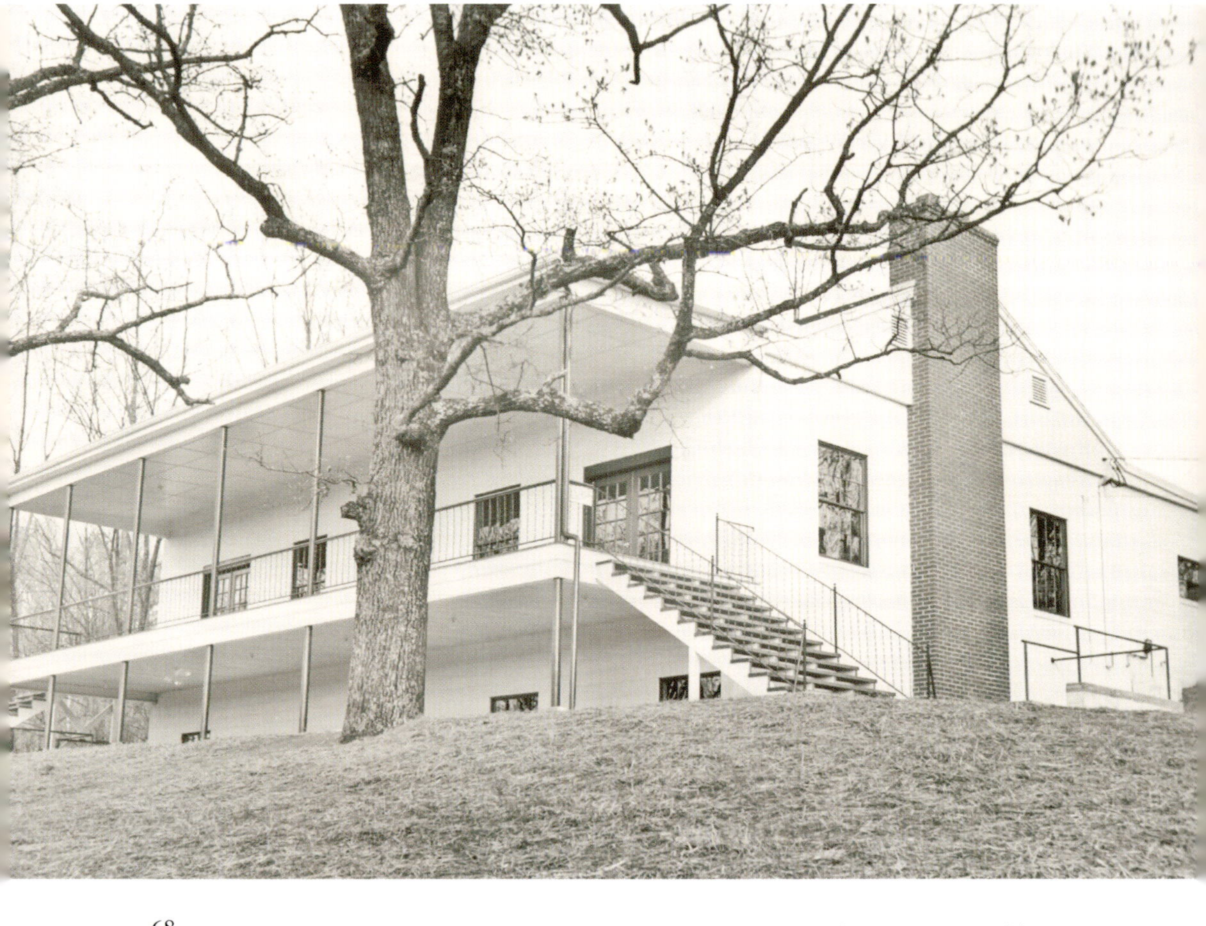

CHAPTER

HOUSES

LIVED IN AND LOVED IN

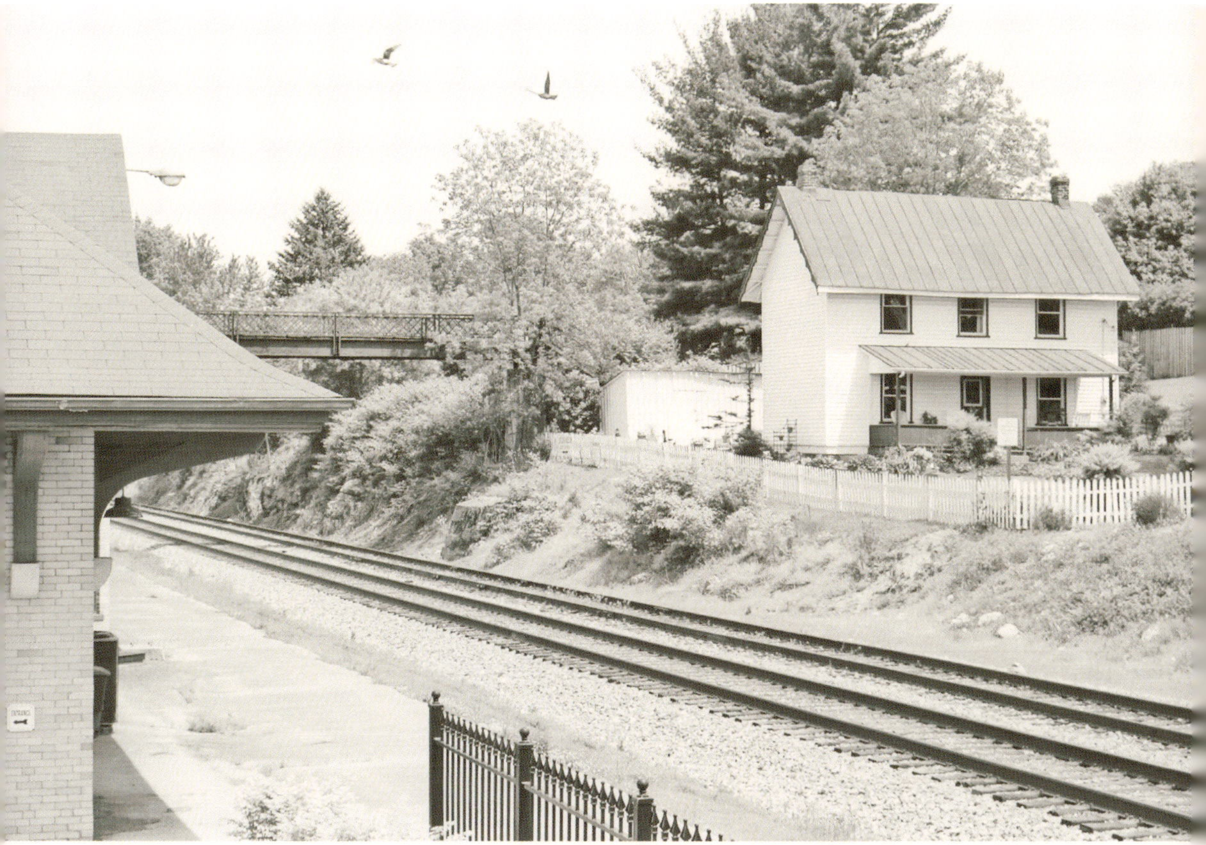

SECTION FOREMAN'S HOUSE. The surviving original building from the depot, the section foreman's house was built in 1854–1857, during the construction of the Virginia and Tennessee Railroad. Afterwards, the section foreman lived there to oversee the maintenance of the line. Although the first Abingdon Depot (1857) burned during the 1864 Stoneman's Raid, this building with its added Gothic Revival–style details has endured and still stands guard by the tracks. The house is being used for a bed and breakfast. (Lynda Campbell and Michael Worrell.)

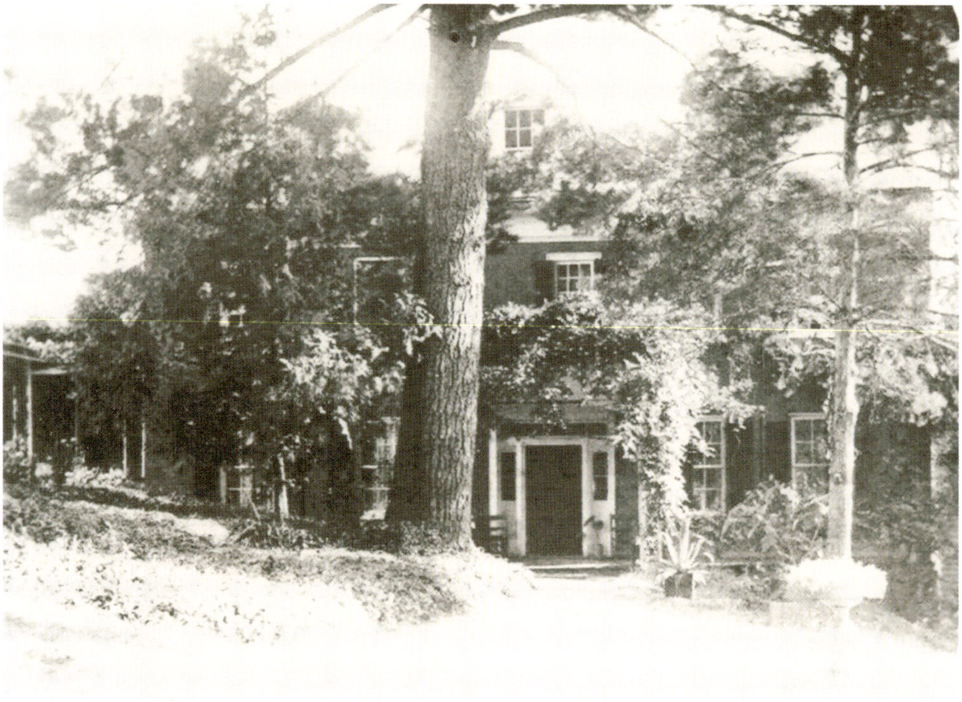

Retirement. Built between 1813 and 1815 by Capt. Robert Craig, this venerable Federal-style brick house, named "Retirement," and its grounds have seen much history and were the site of a silk mill and a muster grounds for local troops from the Revolutionary War to World War I. Located on Colonial Road, this house was used as a residence for many years and in 2007 was purchased by the Town of Abingdon to become part of the trailhead of the National Park Service's Overmountain Victory National Historic Trail. (Then, Garrett Jackson and the Historical Society of Washington County; now, Michael Worrell.)

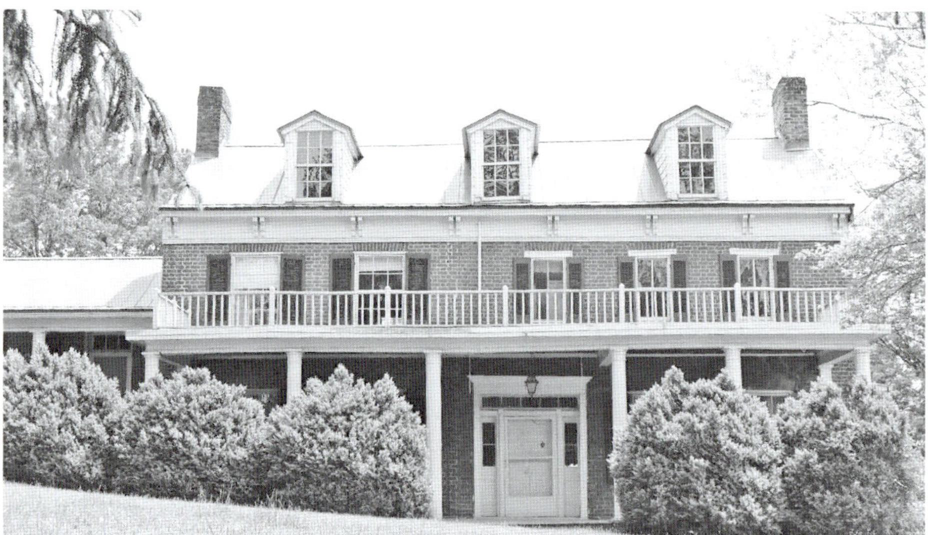

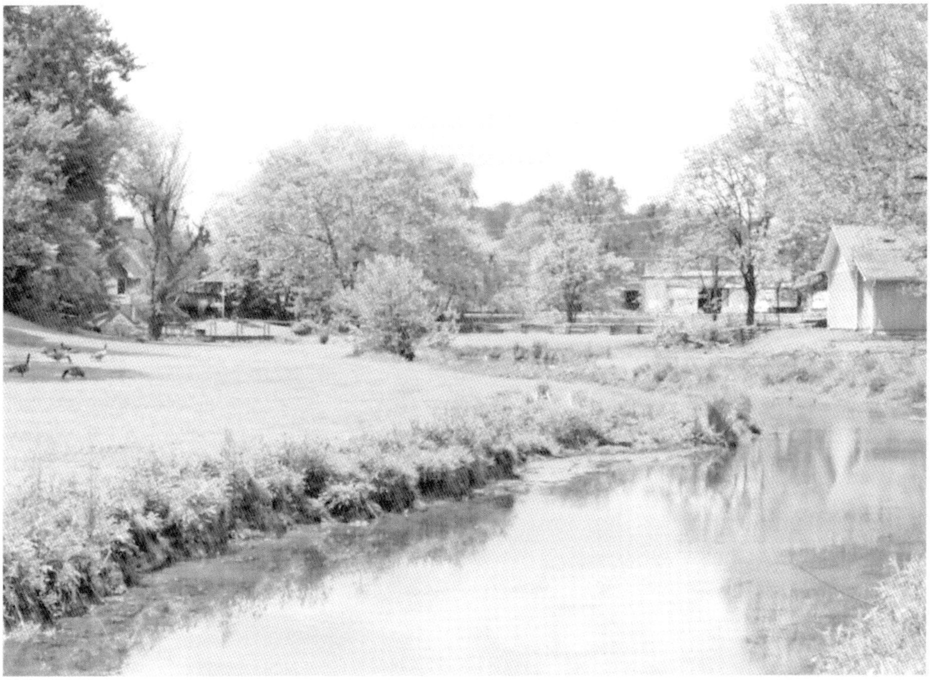

Muster Grounds on Wolf Creek. Retirement, a historic brick house, and the adjoining land were purchased in 2007 by the Town of Abingdon to develop a visitors' center. It is currently being developed as an interpretive site and trailhead of the Overmountain Victory National Historic Trail (part of the National Park Service). This land was used as the muster grounds for each conflict from the Revolutionary War to World War I. (Then, Rick Humphries and Garrett Jackson; now, Michael Worrell.)

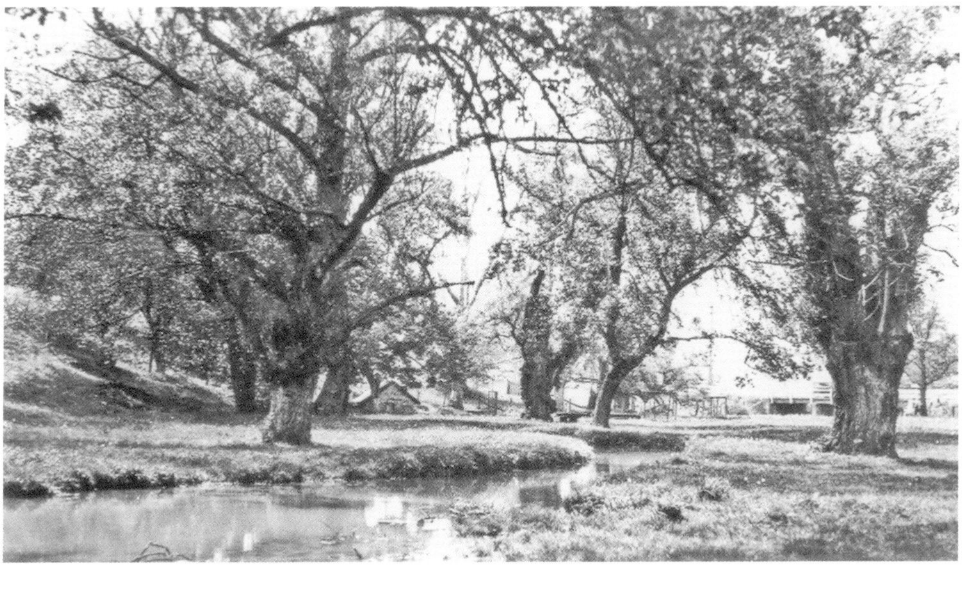

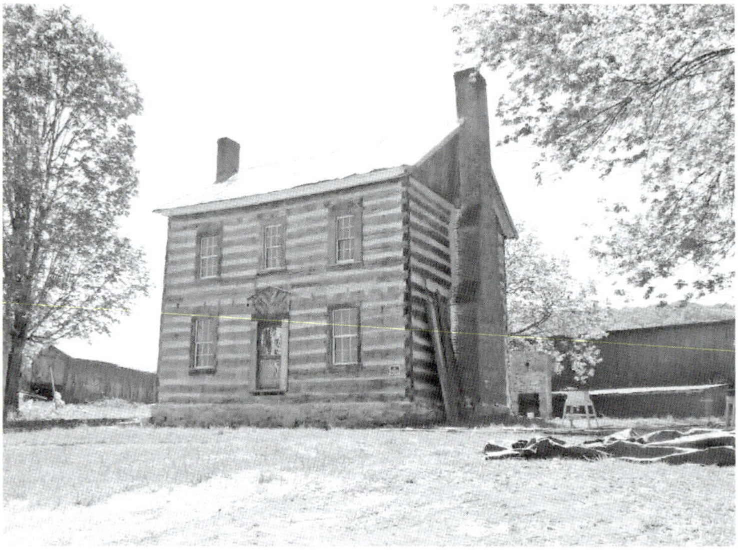

Hagey House. The cladding on the Hagey house covered a log cabin that has stood on Hillman Highway since the early 1800s. Donated to the Town of Abingdon, the log cabin is being restored, and the site is planned for an agricultural incubator and event facility. In the *c.* 1898 photograph below are, from left to right, Jim Hagy, Mary Hagy, William Hagy, and Alma Clark. The Hagys were prominent landowners and began the Hagy Wagon Company and other local businesses. (Then, Juanita Mock Neese; now, Sean Taylor.)

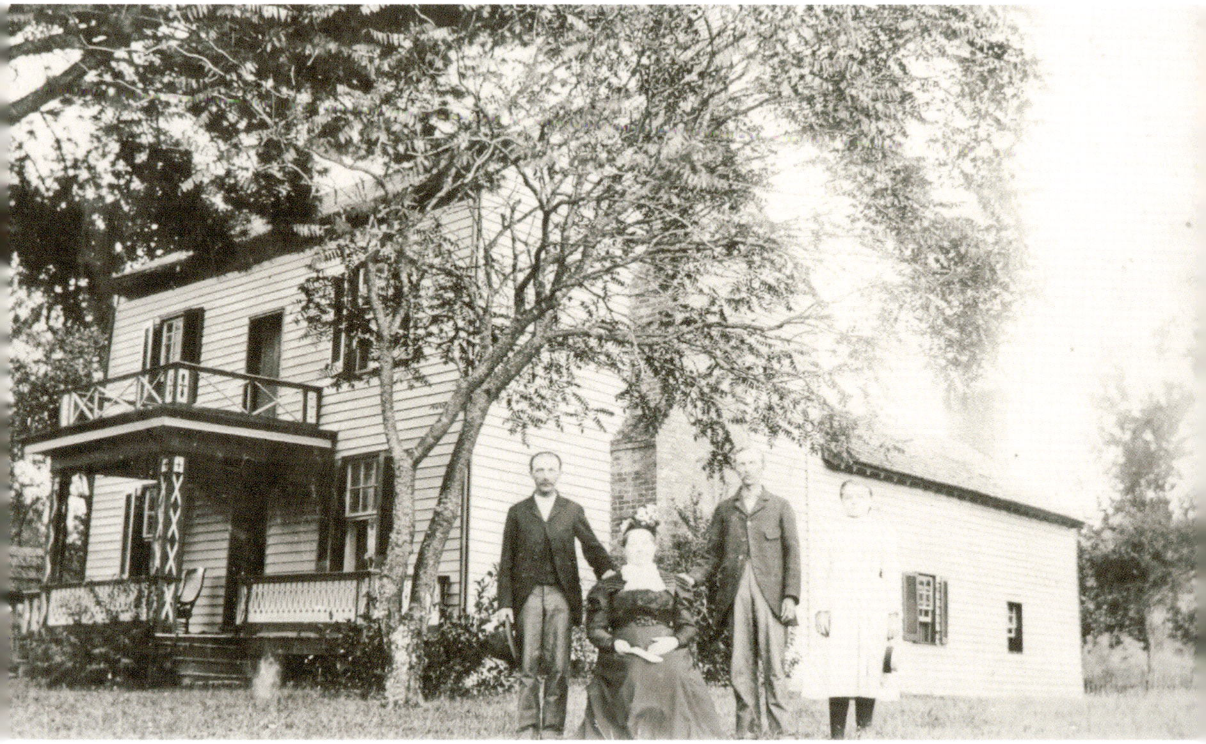

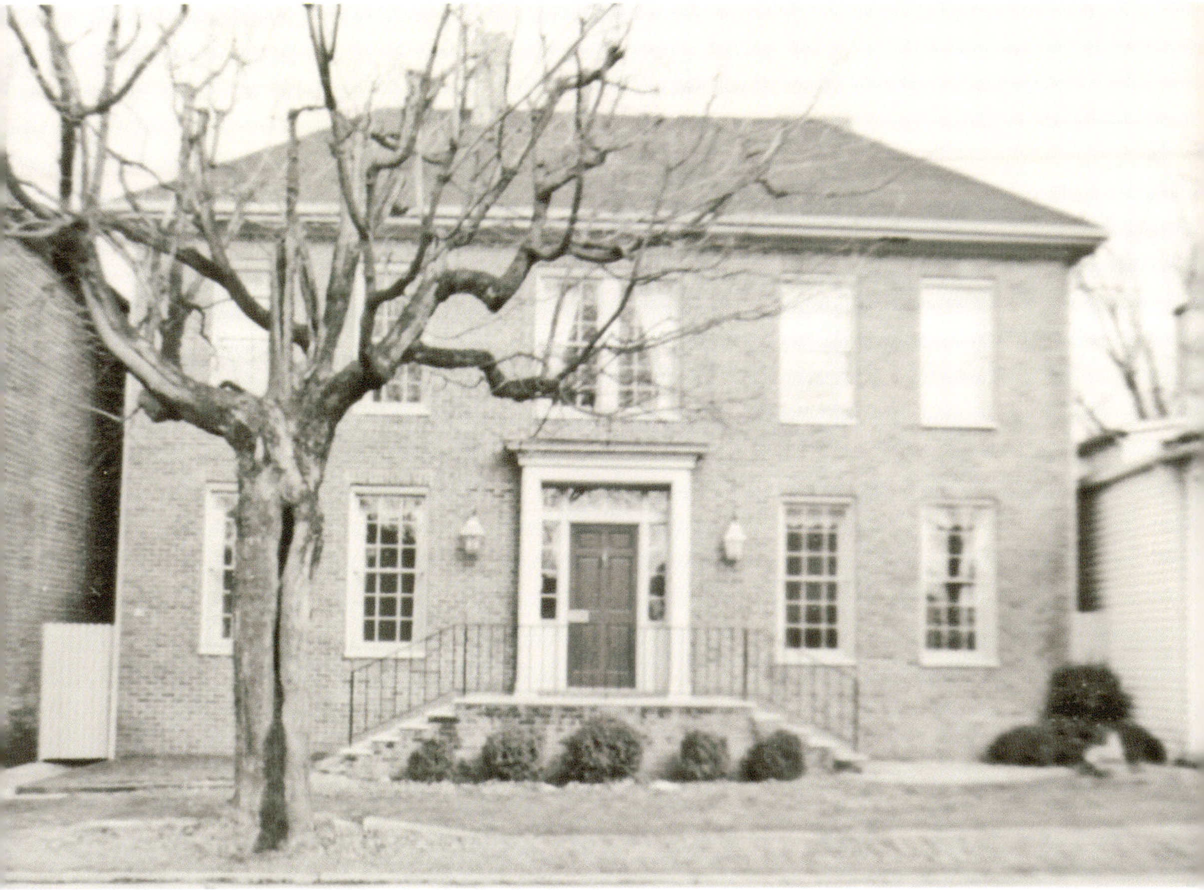

REVEREND ROHR HOUSE. The Reverend Phillip Rohr, a Methodist minister who owned property in the area and in Bristol, built this brick house as a residence in 1845. These two photographs show its excellent preservation and maintenance. Later uses for the building included a millinery shop, a doctor's office, and the town library. The house is currently used for a residence. (Town of Abingdon.)

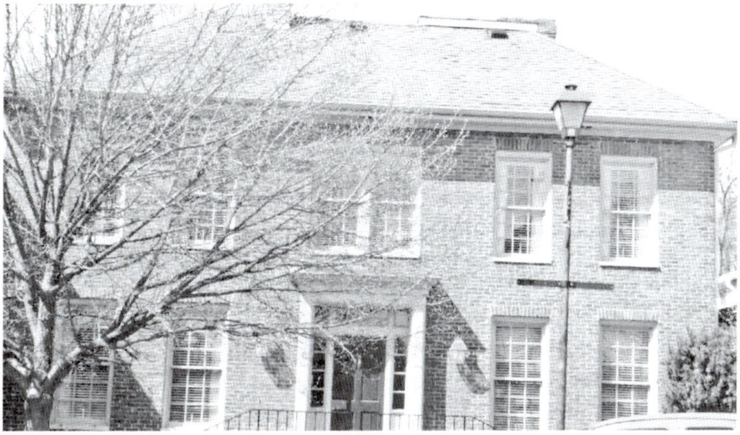

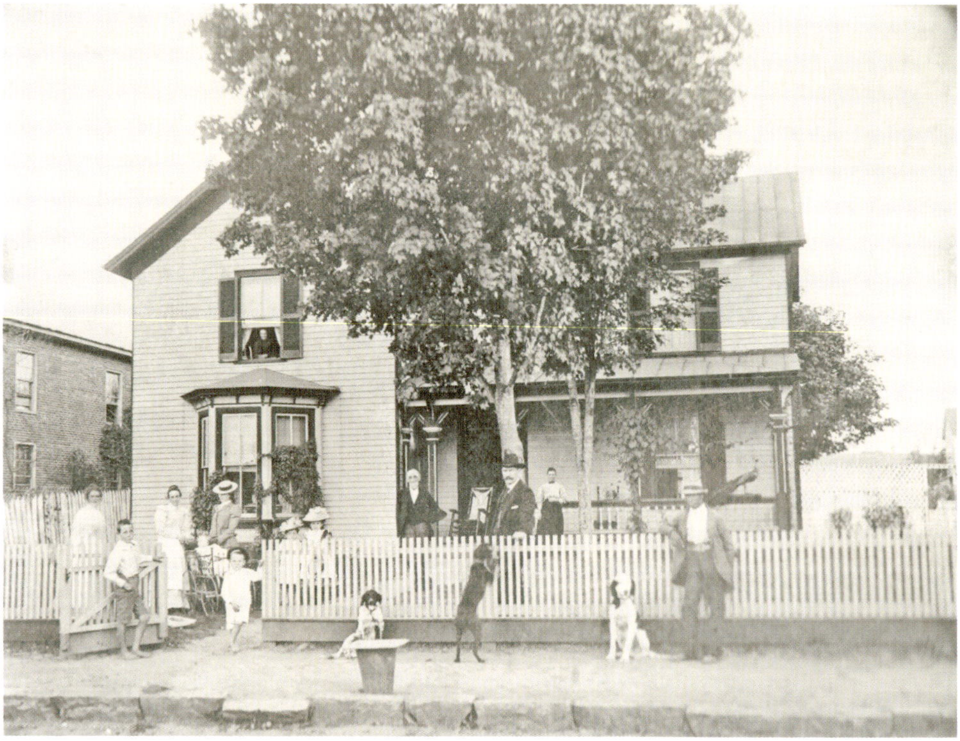

Mahaffey House. Located on the corner of Deadmore and Main Streets, this frame house constructed by James Fields is shown above around 1900. This was one of several houses constructed on the tracts that were sold to early developers. Fields built several of those houses and provided brick for construction. The house was demolished and the current utilitarian brick building served first as a utility office and now a Virginia Lottery office. (Verna Lowe Mahaffey.)

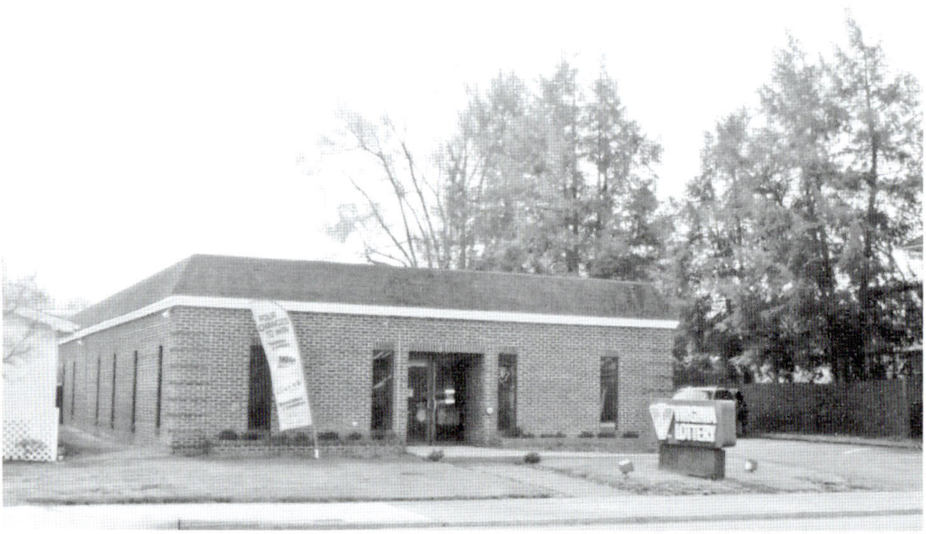

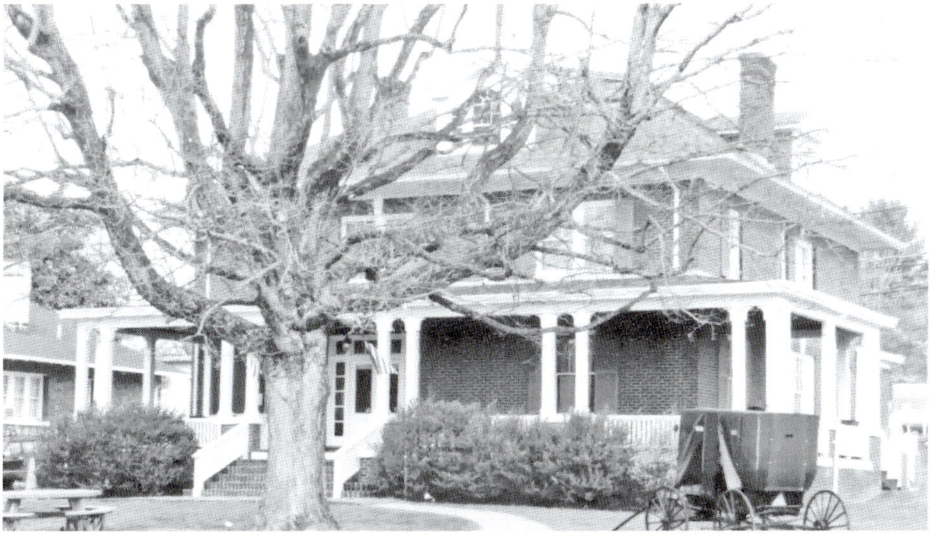

SAMUEL A. CARSON HOUSE. Known as the Moore Music House and shown below around 1965, this expansive house was built in 1909 by W. H. Musser for Samuel and Lelia Carson. Carson was a local business owner and partner in the Hamilton-Carson store, located west of the house on Main Street. Most recently, the house has reopened as an upscale restaurant, a welcome addition for downtown diners. (Town of Abingdon.)

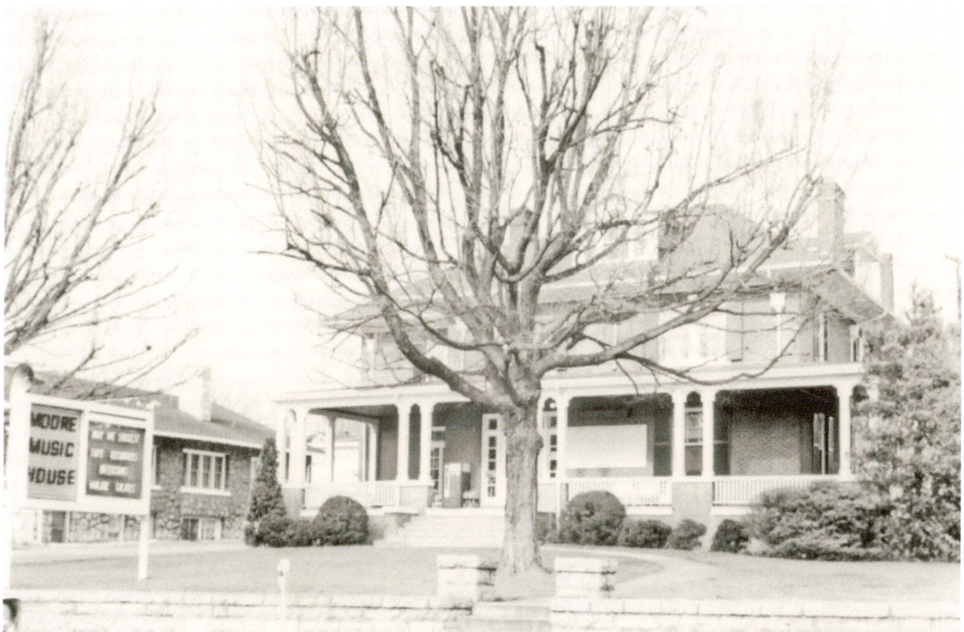

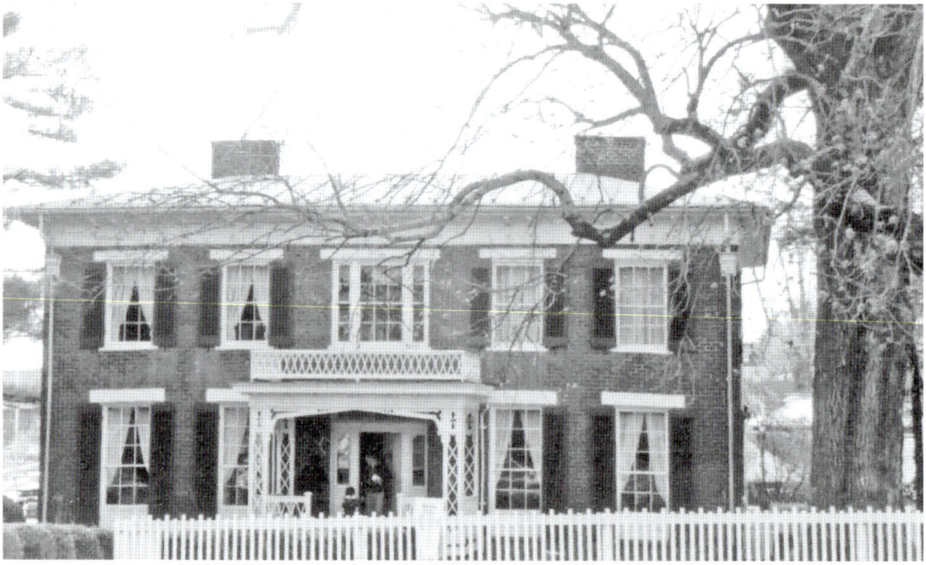

Fields-Penn House. In 1858, James Fields built this house with a blend of Greek Revival and Italianate styles for his own residence. George Penn, a lawyer who established a well-known law firm, was the next owner in the late 1800s. Fortunately, the handsome house was saved from likely demolition when a foundation purchased it. The building has now been restored and is a house museum operated by the William King Regional Arts Center. (Peggy Johnson.)

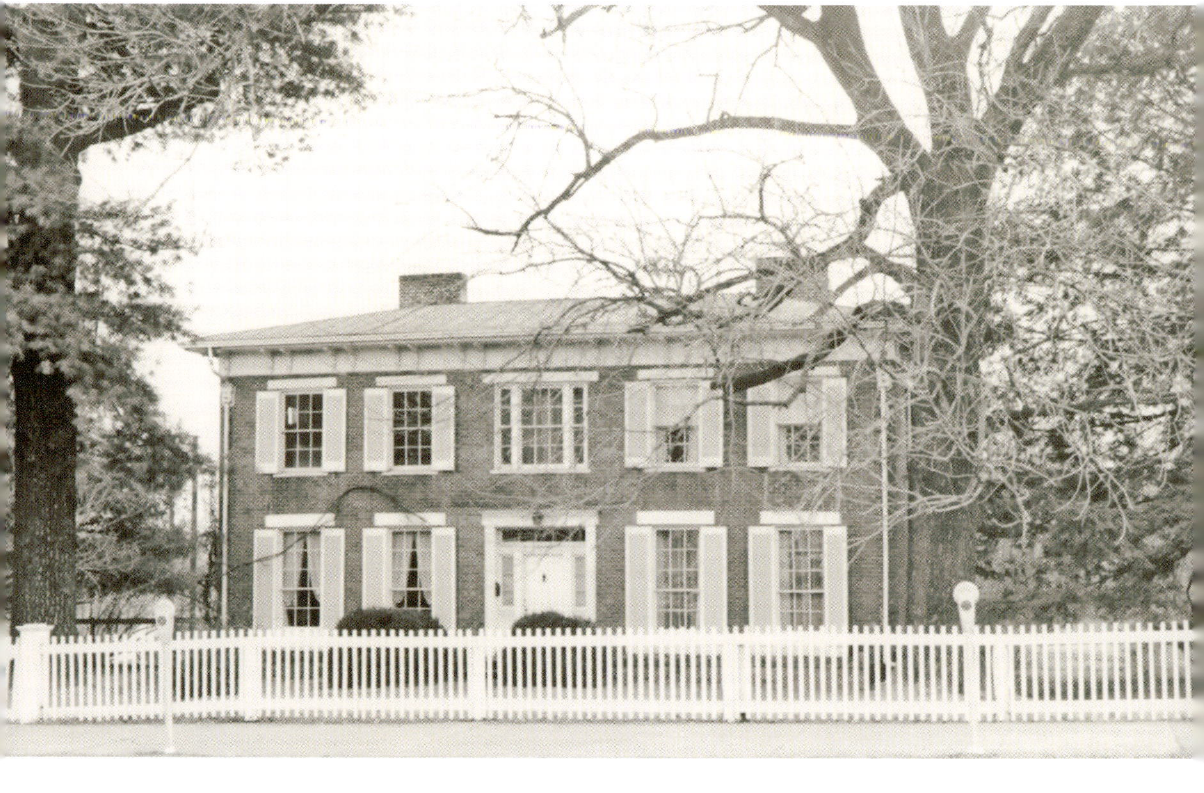

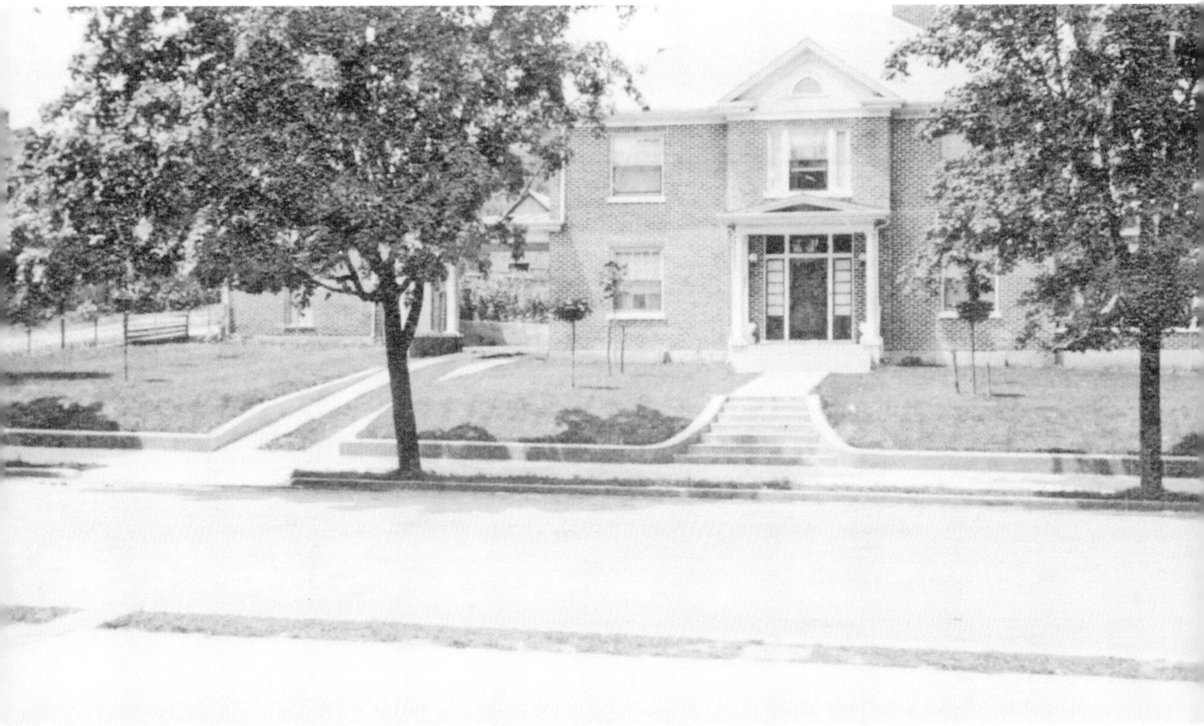

Honaker House. Although two earlier houses occupied this lot at the desirable intersection of Cummings and Main Streets, the present house was built by A. Chris Honaker in 1917. The earlier houses were used for a dental office and were residences for several local ministers. As the *c.* 1917 photograph above shows, what was originally the side yard of the house is now a lane to Cummings Street added in the late 1960s. (Jimmie Lou Moore Bowden.)

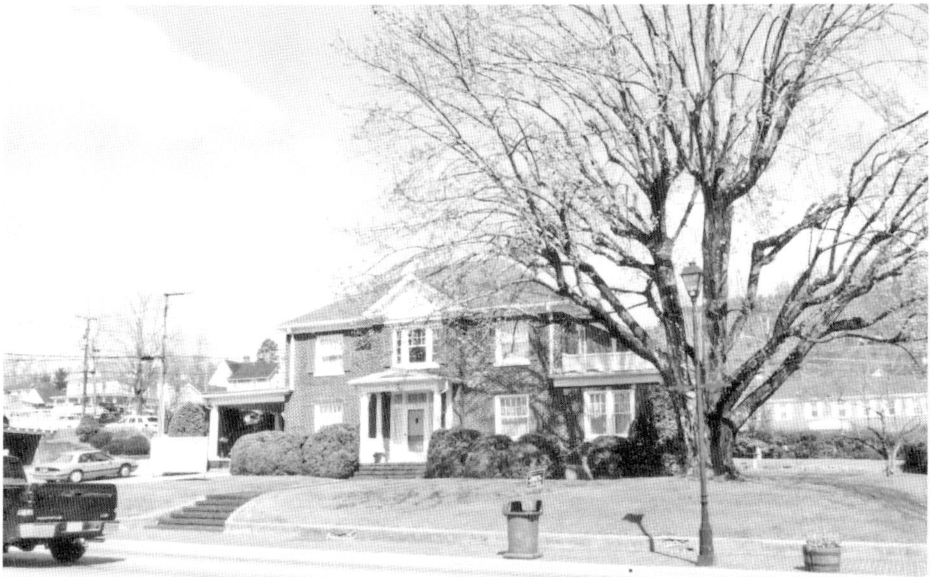

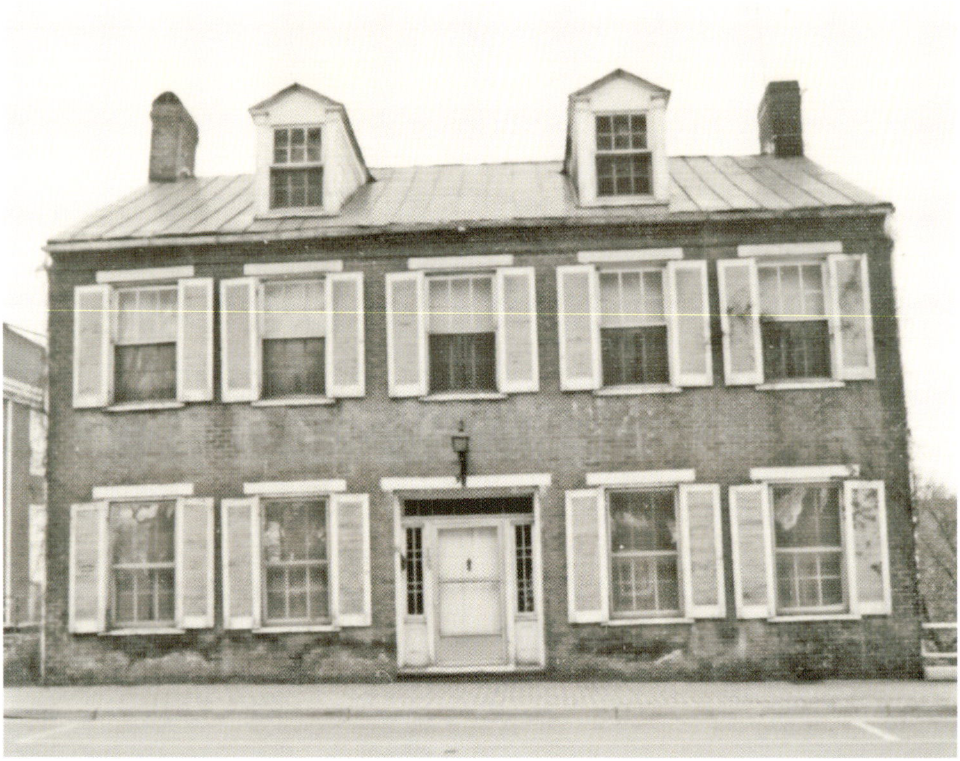

William Rodefer House. Shown in 1973, this Main Street residence was built by William Rodefer after 1856. The house is an excellent example of the Federal style, popular in the early 19th century. Rodefer also built the Colonnade Hotel, which was previously located on Main Street near the courthouse. (Town of Abingdon.)

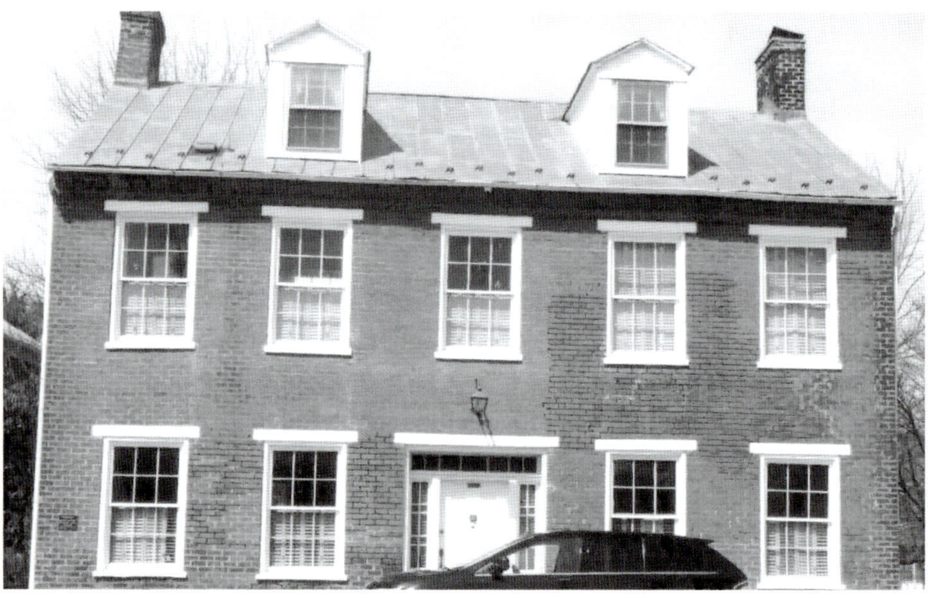

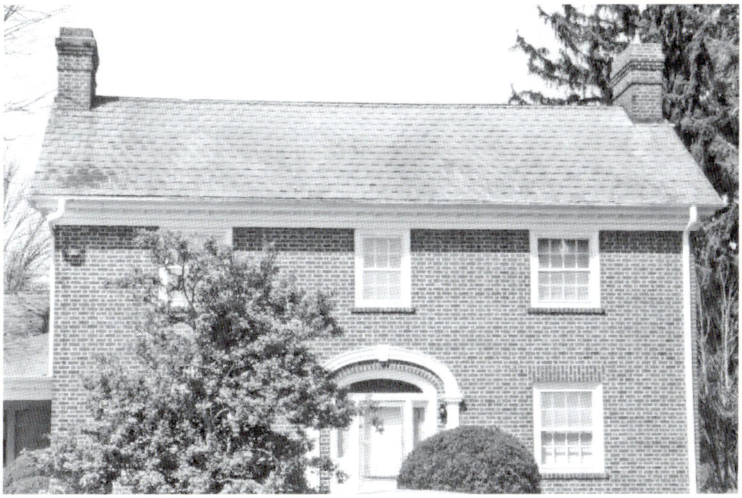

Shipley House. Built in 1938 by J. L. Shipley, this building was not the first on the lot. A 1798 log house and blacksmith shop occupied this lot, and in 1872, James A. Hagy purchased the lot and the adjacent one and built a new house, adding several buildings and operating the Hagy Wagon Factory here until the business was moved to Floyd and Preston Streets near the railroad. A general store was also operated on the corner lot, and a primary school occupied the second floor in 1907. (Town of Abingdon.)

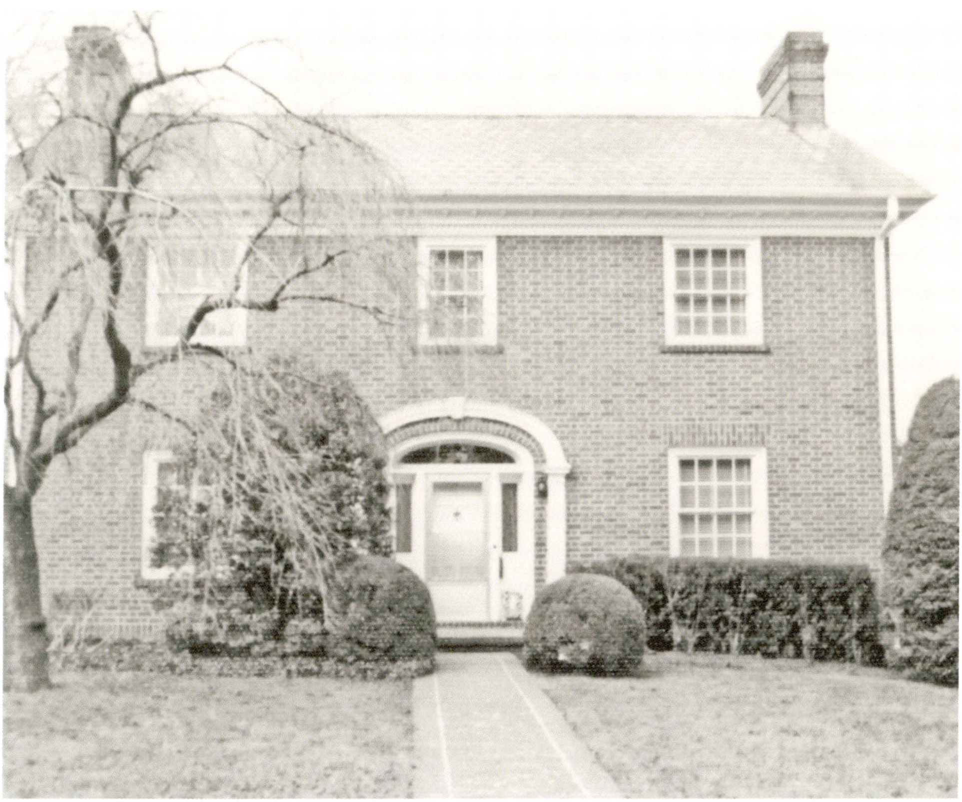

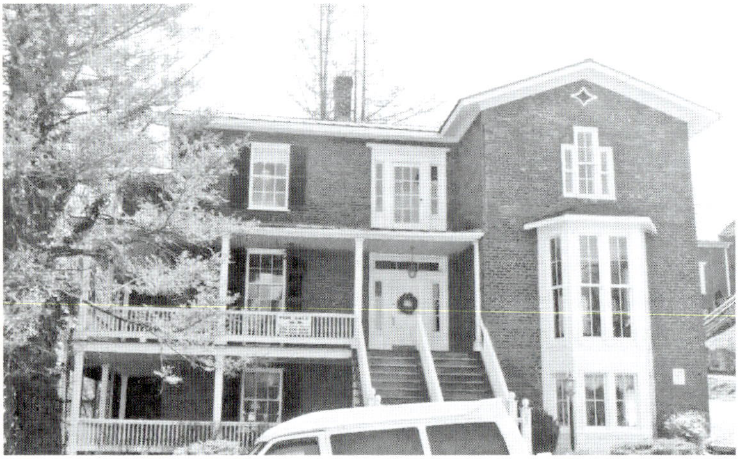

Barr House. As shown in the 1972 photograph below, the Barr house has been located on East Main Street since 1871. John W. Barr built this house, but previously the land was owned by Michael Shaver, a distinguished silversmith in the early 1800s, and used for a blacksmith shop, a tavern, and residence. Those buildings were destroyed in the 1856 fire, and Barr built this house and two others in this block. It is located adjacent to the Barter Playhouse and is used for a residence. (Town of Abingdon.)

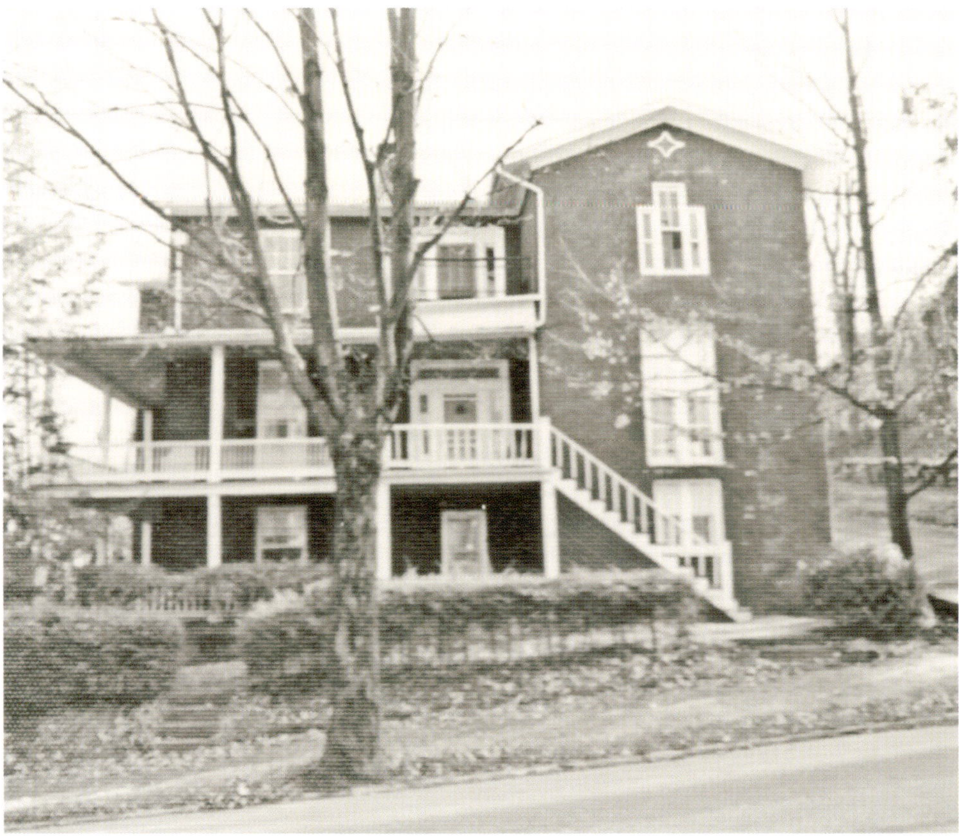

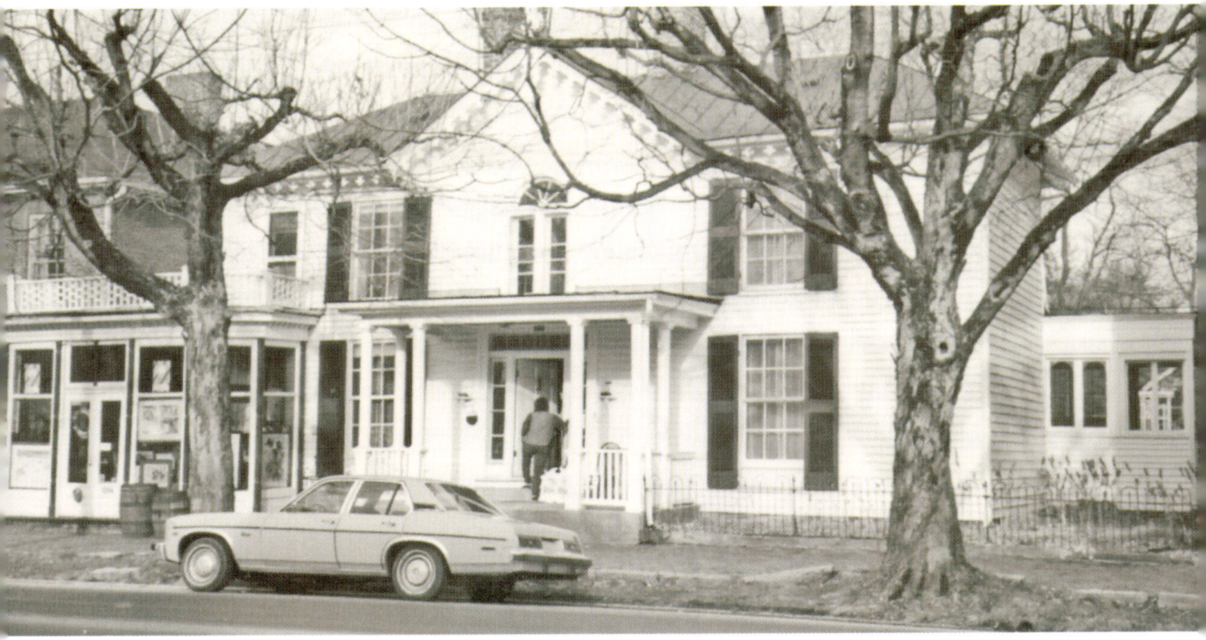

BAUGH HOUSE. This house dates back to 1807, when Valentine Baugh built an addition to a log cabin and added the wood siding. He purchased the eastern portion of the lot to add to the house. Baugh was a respected surveyor and postmaster, and he published the *Abingdon Democrat* newspaper beginning in 1849. Presently, the house is used as a residence and a retail clothing store. (Town of Abingdon.)

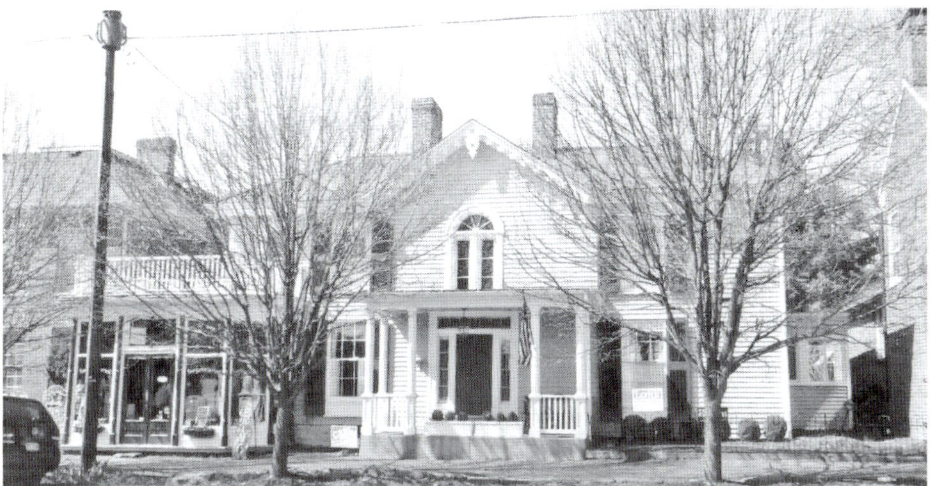

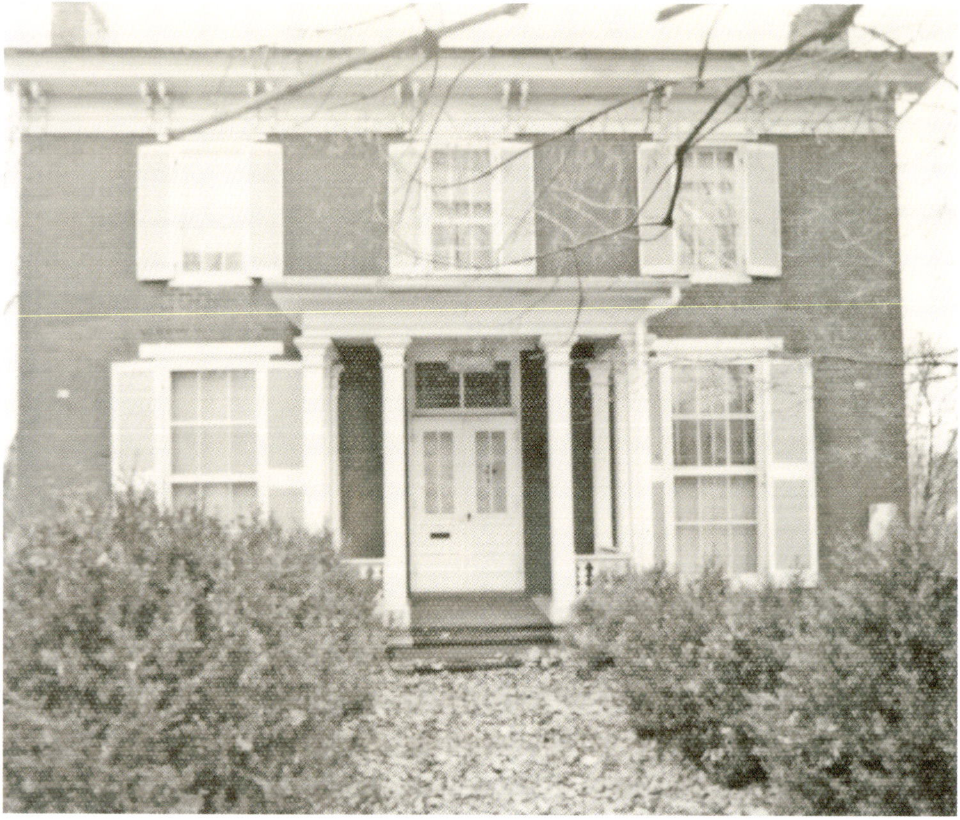

ANDREW GIBSON HOUSE. Located near the intersection of Pecan and Main Streets, the front section of this brick house was built in 1836 by Andrew Gibson, a former mayor of Abingdon. The rear section was added by John G. Kreger in 1875. Kreger is considered a hero of Abingdon because he removed the town records from the courthouse during the Civil War to protect the official papers. (Town of Abingdon.)

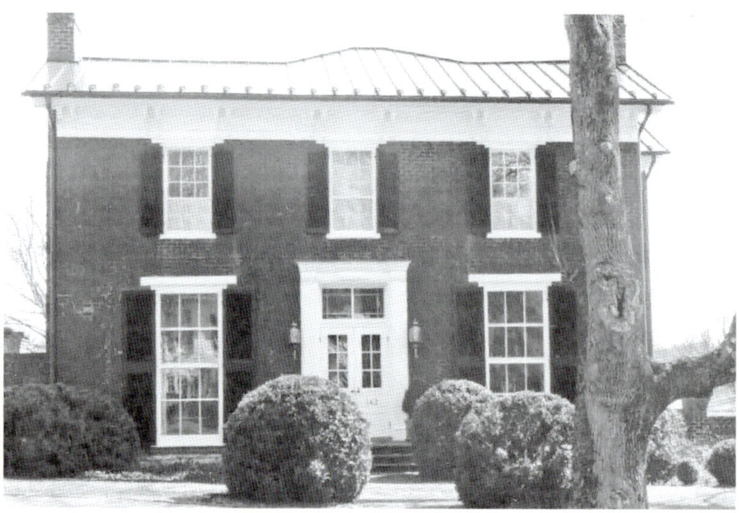

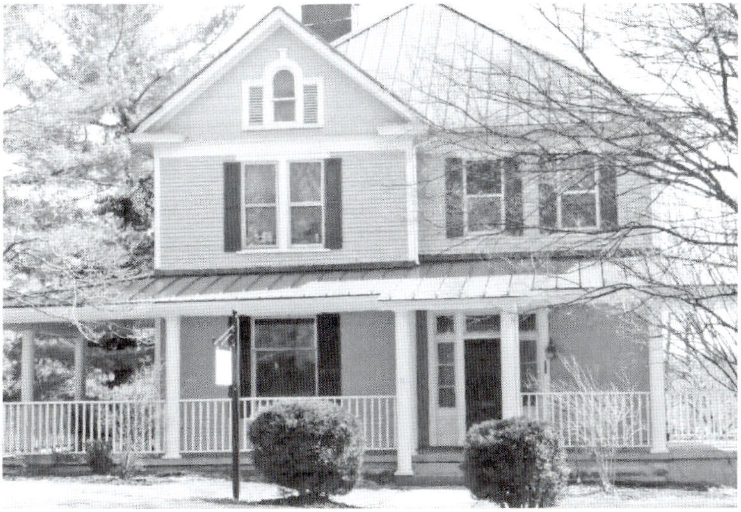

EPISCOPAL RECTORY. Although a log cabin previously occupied this lot, the St. Thomas Episcopal Church built this house in 1908, and it was used for a rectory until 1942. The 1972 photograph below shows how different the house appeared compared to the present. The columns and widow's walk didn't flatter the building, and its restoration was a wise decision by property owners. (Town of Abingdon.)

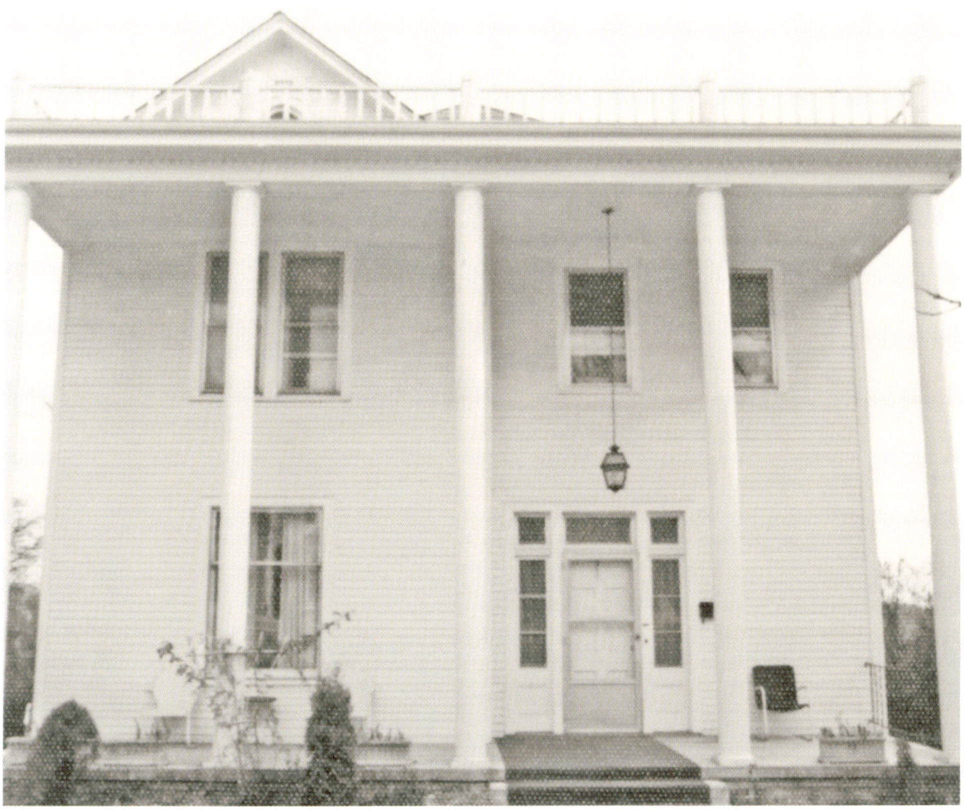

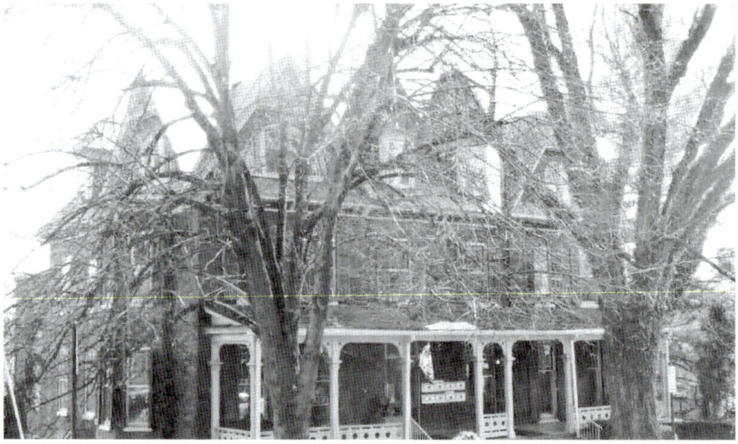

Greenway-Trigg Building. This lovely three-story brick house was built as a duplex in 1884 for Thomas and Bettie Trigg and James C. and Nannie Greenway and remained in the families until 1938. It was renovated for offices of the *Washington County News* and now houses retail shops and offices. (Town of Abingdon.)

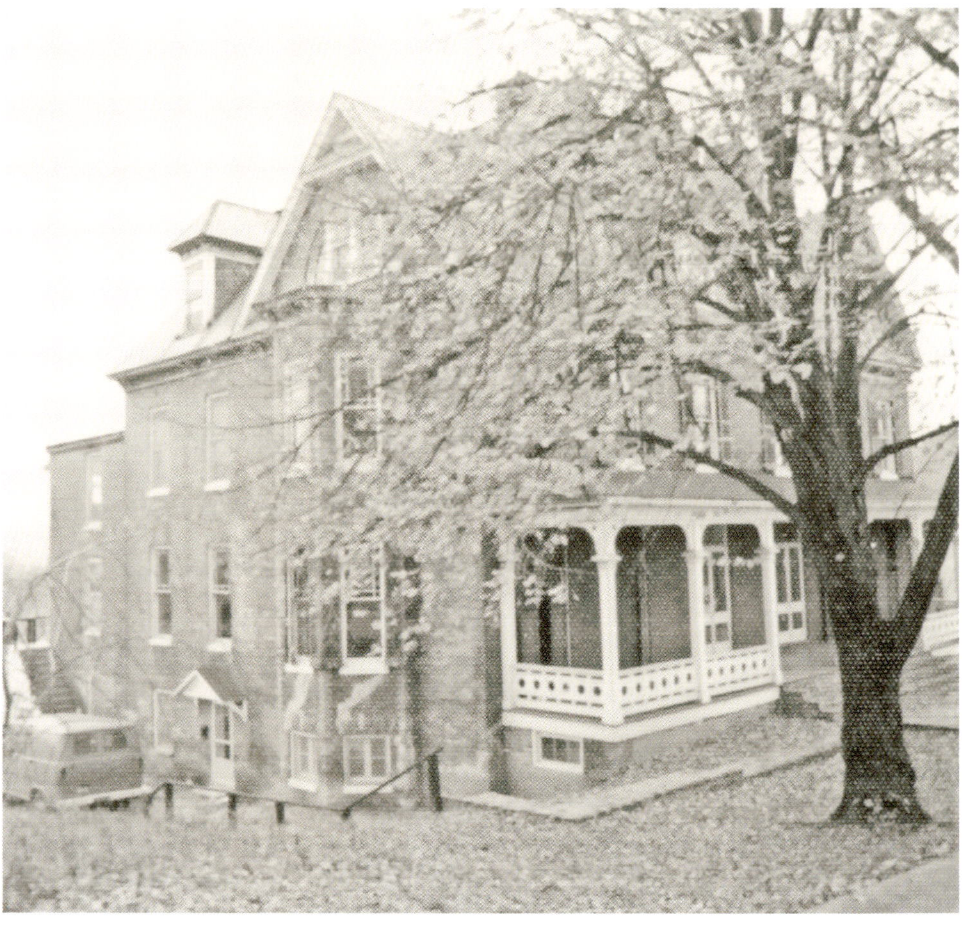

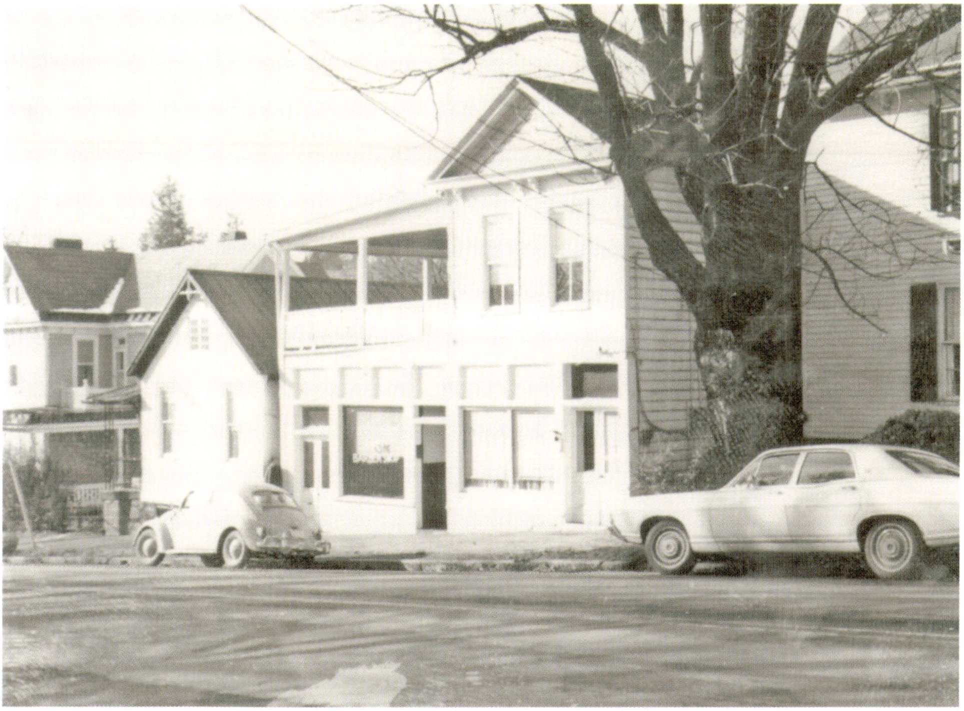

RENCHER HOUSE AND BARBERSHOP. In 1887, John A. Rencher had this frame residence built with a two-story shop in front. Rencher was a popular barber and also ran a public bathhouse here. The Rencher family provided three generations of barbers to the region and drew customers from distant towns. The building underwent renovations, as seen by the differences in the *c.* 1970 image above and the present photograph below, and is now used for offices. (Emmitt F. Yeary.)

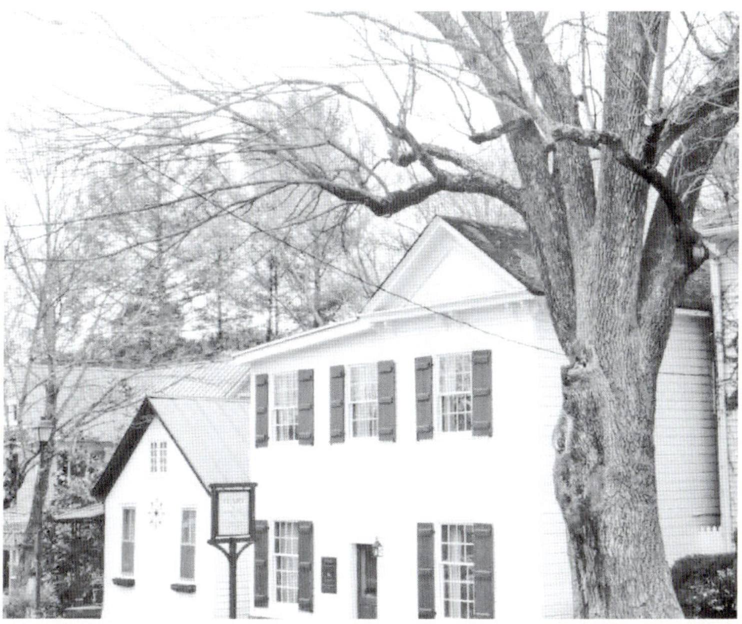

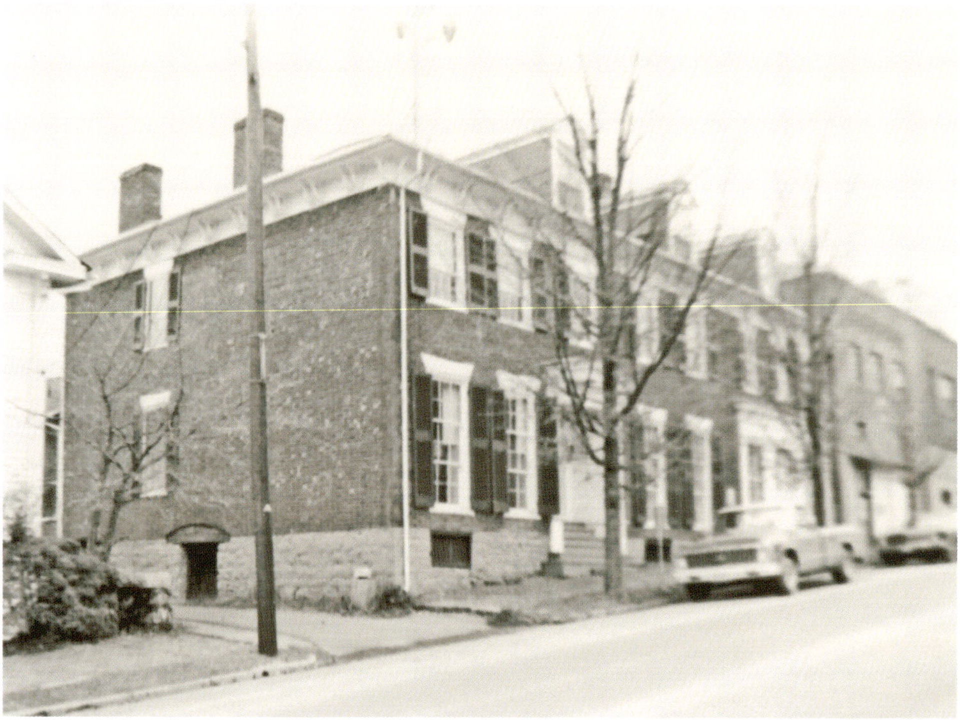

COL. JAMES WHITE HOUSE. Located on Main Street west of the courthouse, this stately brick house was built in 1819, with a store/office addition built to the east in 1828. James White owned a mercantile, a tannery, and iron furnaces, as well as property in other states. During the 1864 Civil War fire that burned the courthouse, the brick house and store were partially burned, but they were restored after the war. The building is currently used for a residence. (Town of Abingdon.)

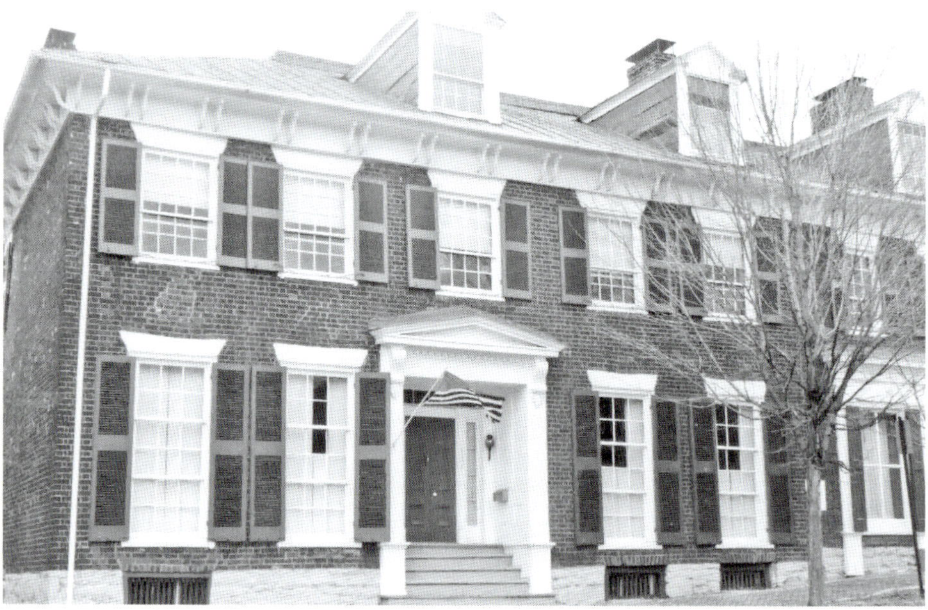

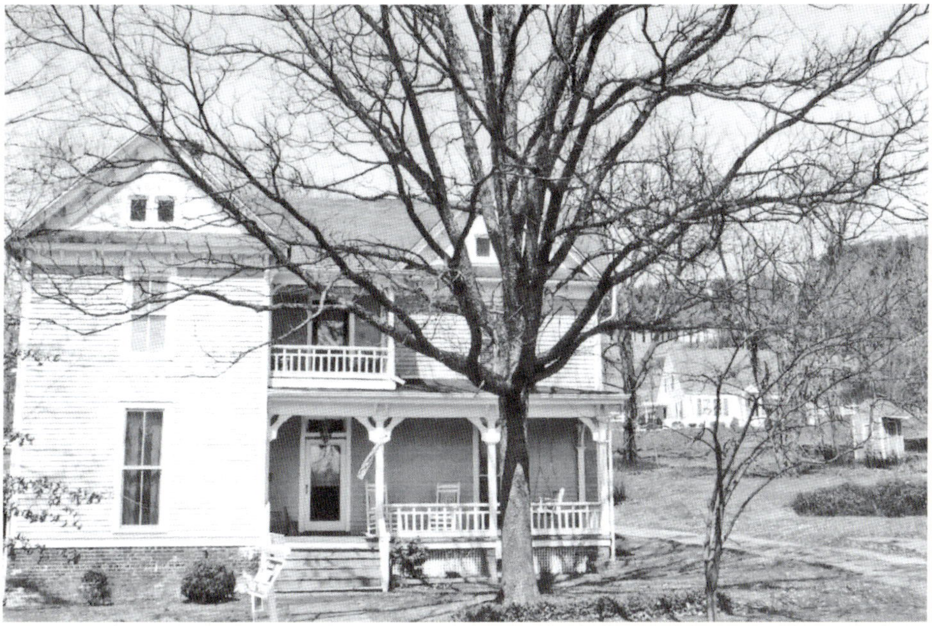

HAMILTON HOUSE. Located on Valley Street, this two-story home with double gables was built in 1895 for Thomas S. Hamilton. The Maiden family owned it for many years and has maintained its historic character and integrity. W. A. Maiden operated Maiden's Drug Store, a popular drugstore and soda fountain, in the downtown area in the early 1900s. Note in the historic photograph below that another house sits to the east that is no longer there. (Edith Maiden Hatcher.)

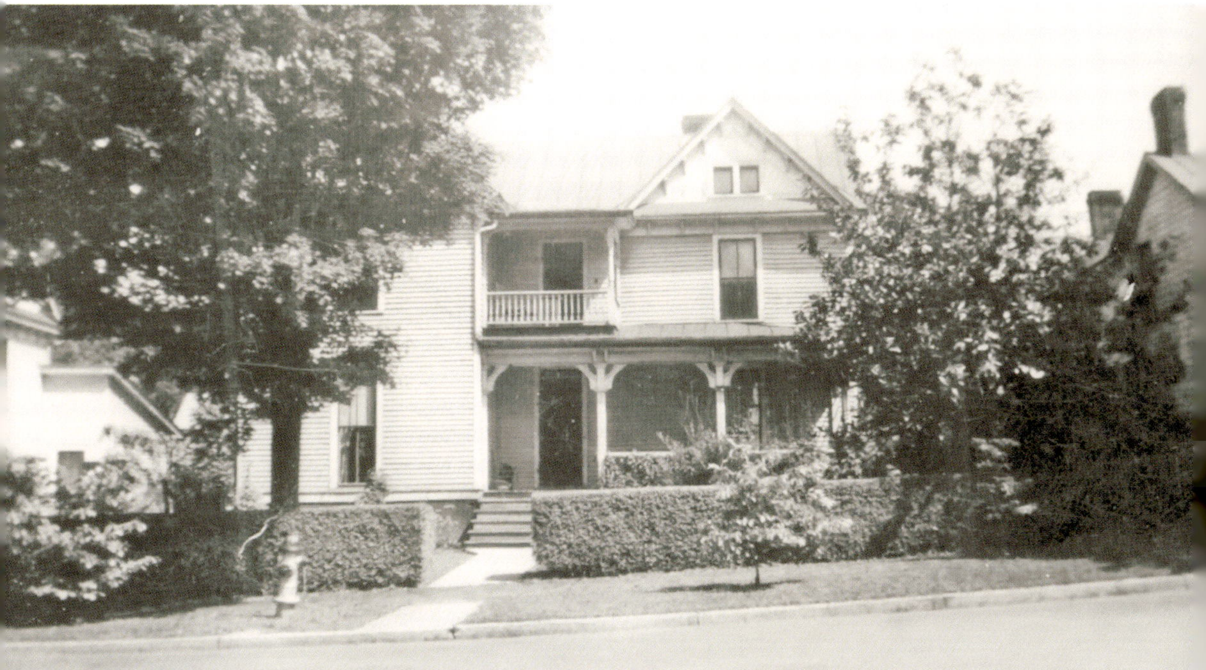

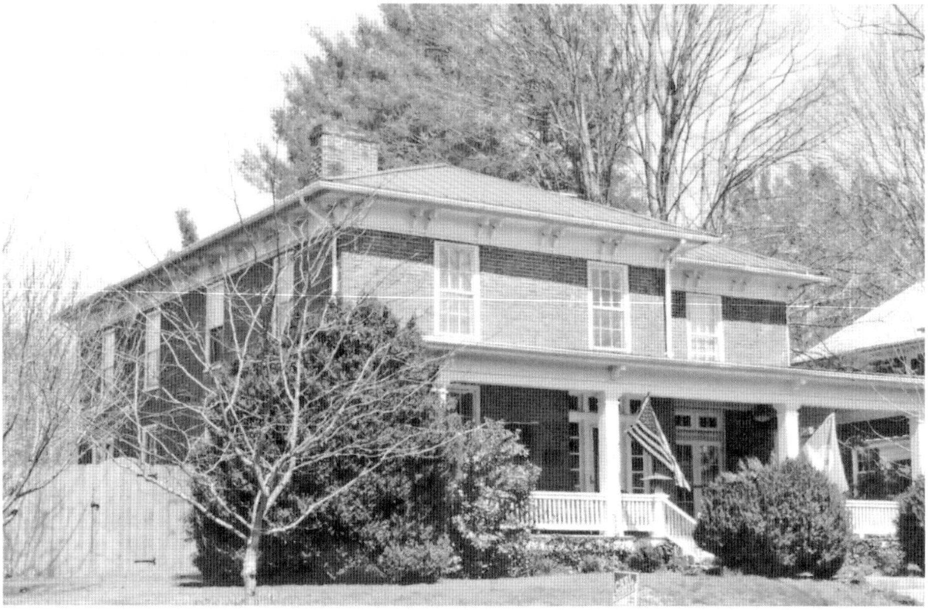

Presbyterian Parsonage. This brick two-story house was built in 1873 by Francis Smith and James Fields for the Sinking Spring Presbyterian Church congregation. The Reverend Edward H. Barnett was the first occupant of the house, and it later became a private residence. This sturdy house has most recently been used as a bed and breakfast. (Town of Abingdon.)

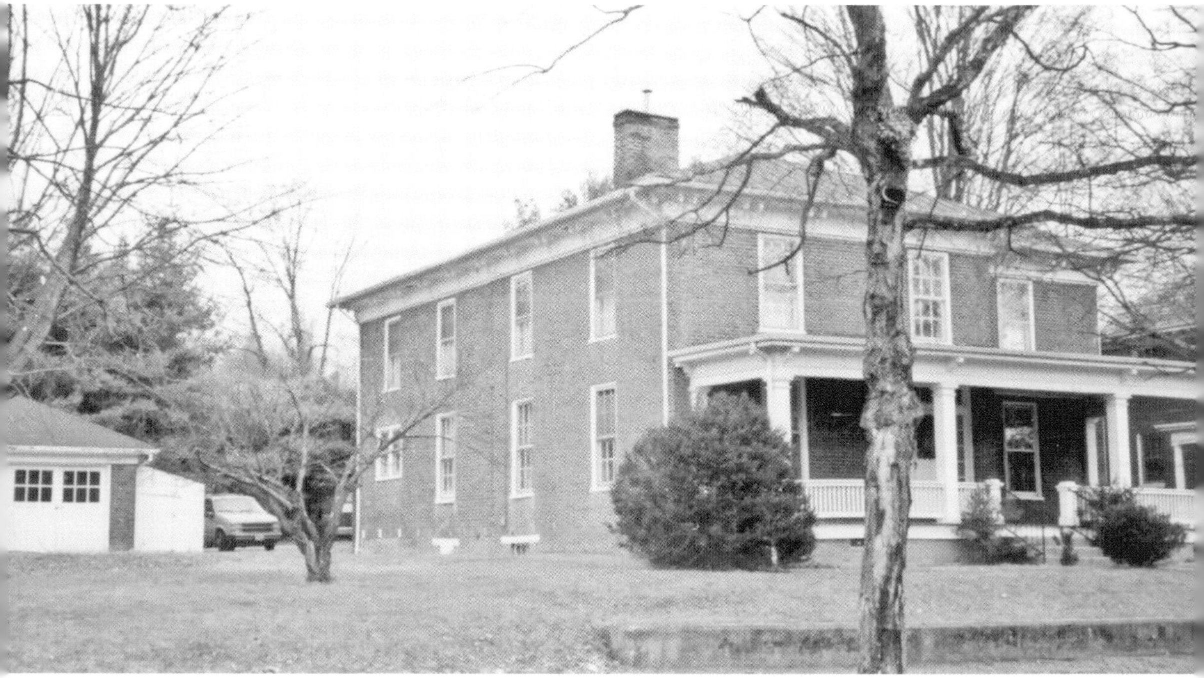

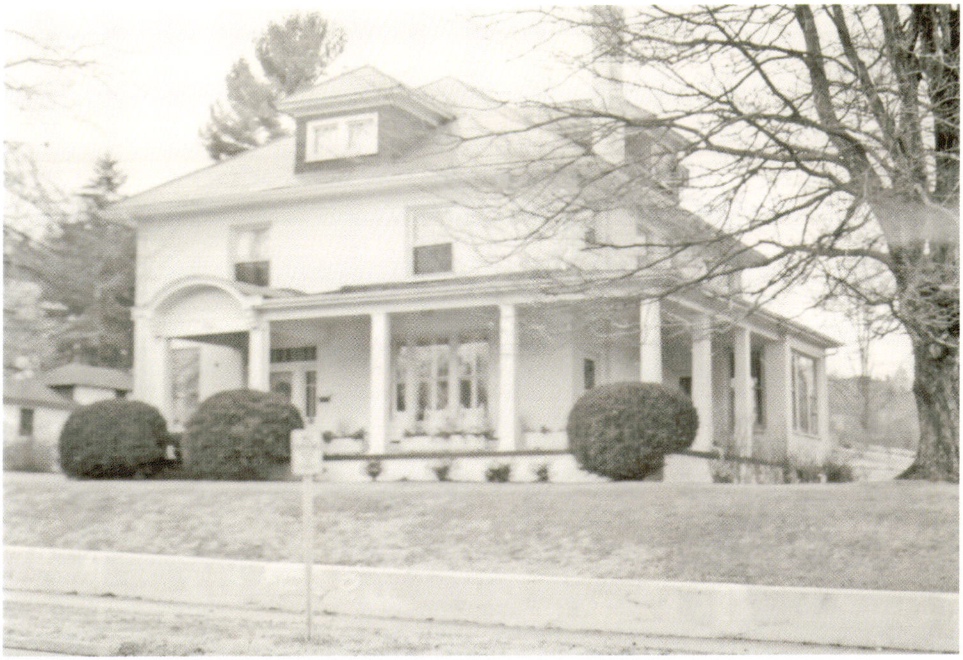

John L. Bradley House. Located on Valley Street, this house was built for John L. and Margaret Jennings Bradley in 1921. The Bradleys were owners of Miller and Bradley, a lumber dealer in Abingdon. After 1927, the house was donated to the Methodist Episcopal church to be used for traveling ministers. The property has been known as the Summerfield Inn, a lovely bed and breakfast establishment, since 1986. (Town of Abingdon.)

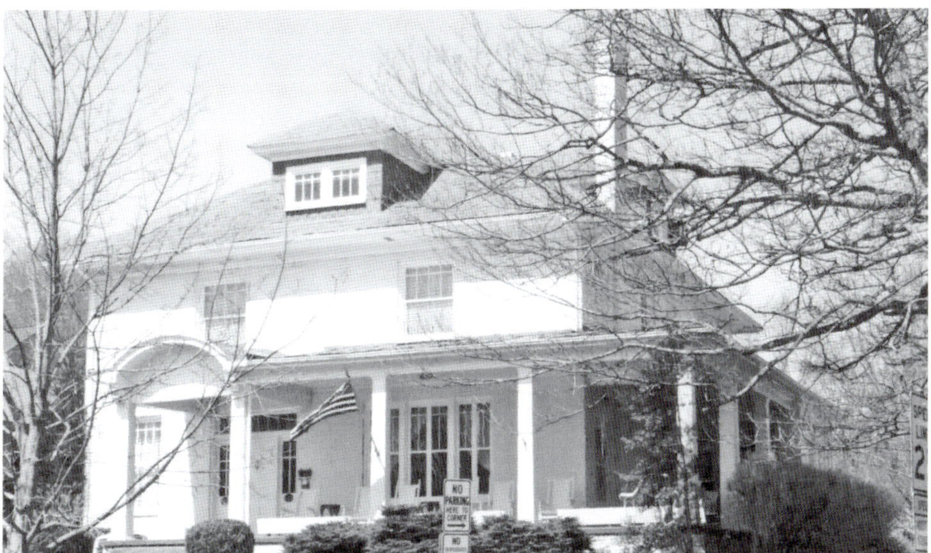

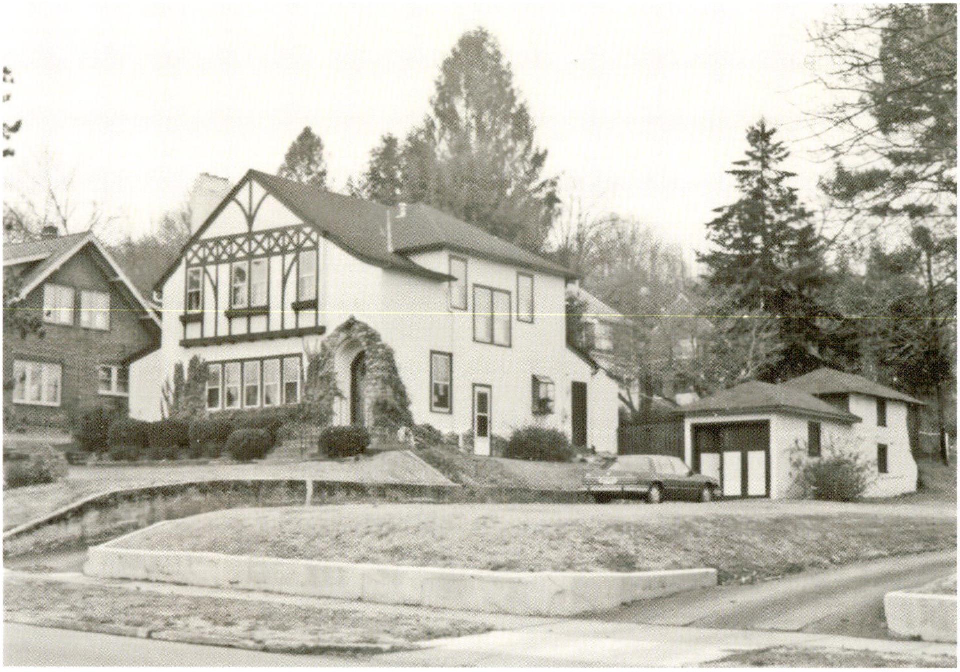

William R. Cline House. Built in 1928 by William R. and Louise Hayter Cline, this house stands out among the houses lining Valley Street. The unique house represents the Medieval Revival architectural style and includes timbering and stonework. Owners have maintained its historic integrity, and it appears to be in excellent condition. (Town of Abingdon.)

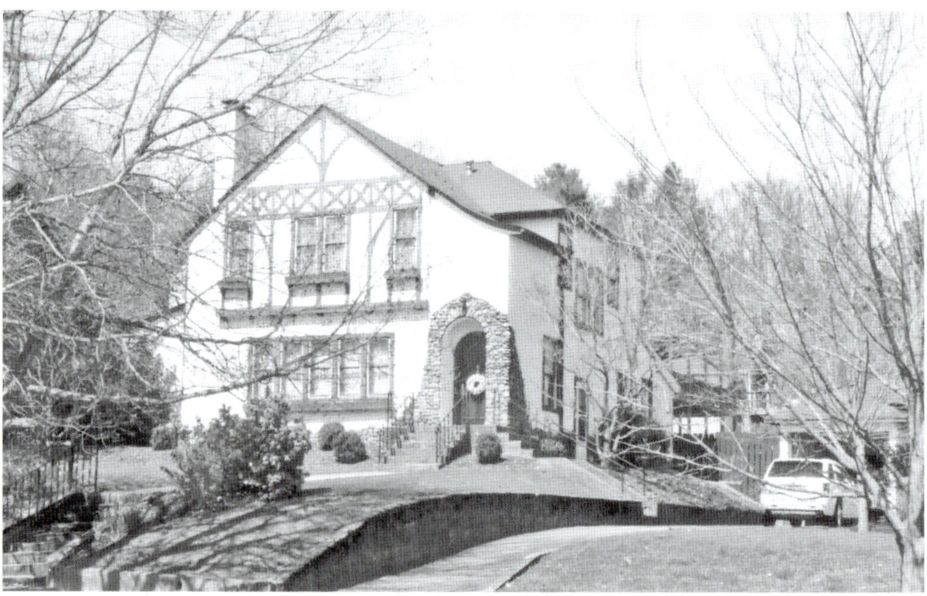

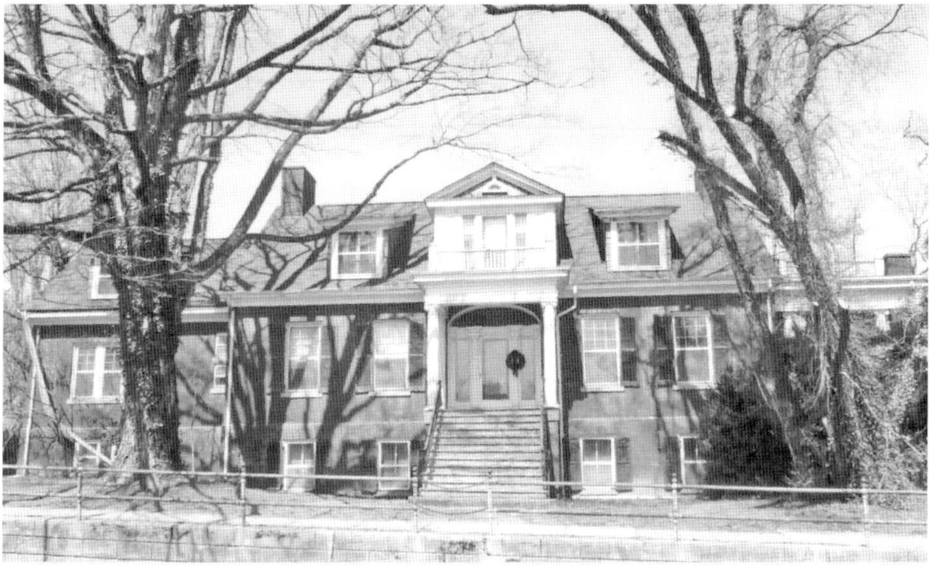

Findlay House. This Federal-style house was built in 1827 for Alexander Findlay, making it one of the earlier houses on Valley Street. Findlay was a successful merchant, property owner, and part owner of a family business mining salt in nearby Saltville. The east and west wings were added later, as was new brickwork over the older central section. The house is in need of maintenance and restoration. (Town of Abingdon.)

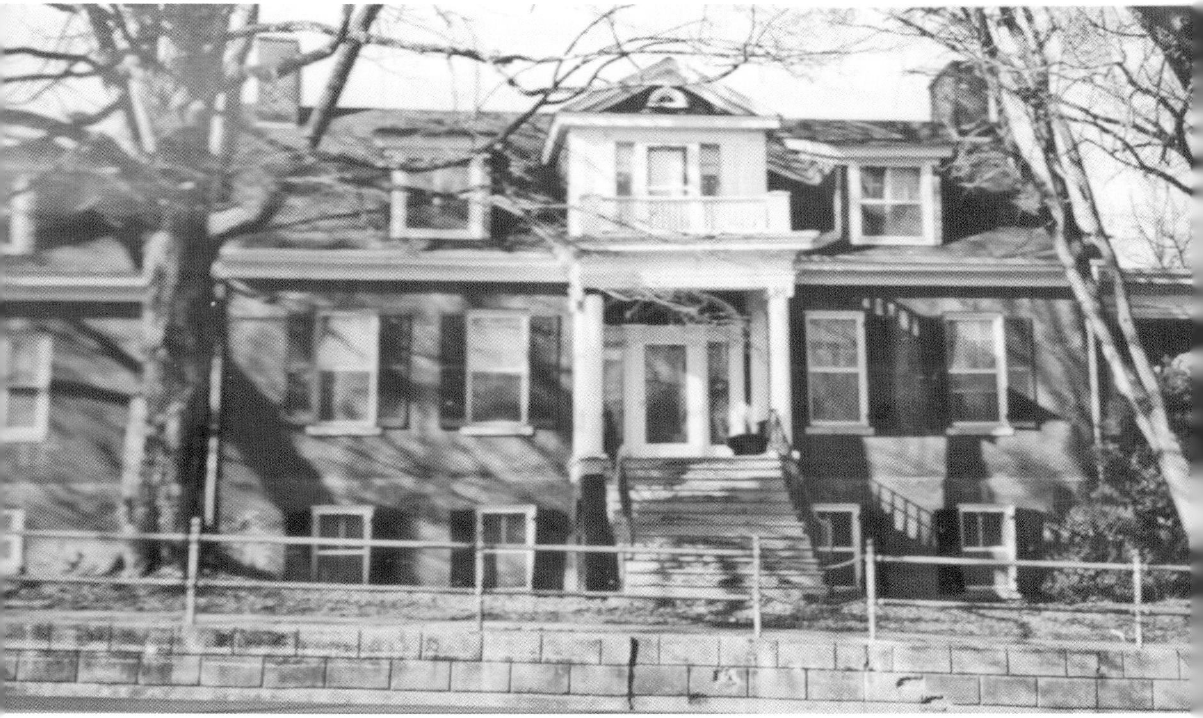

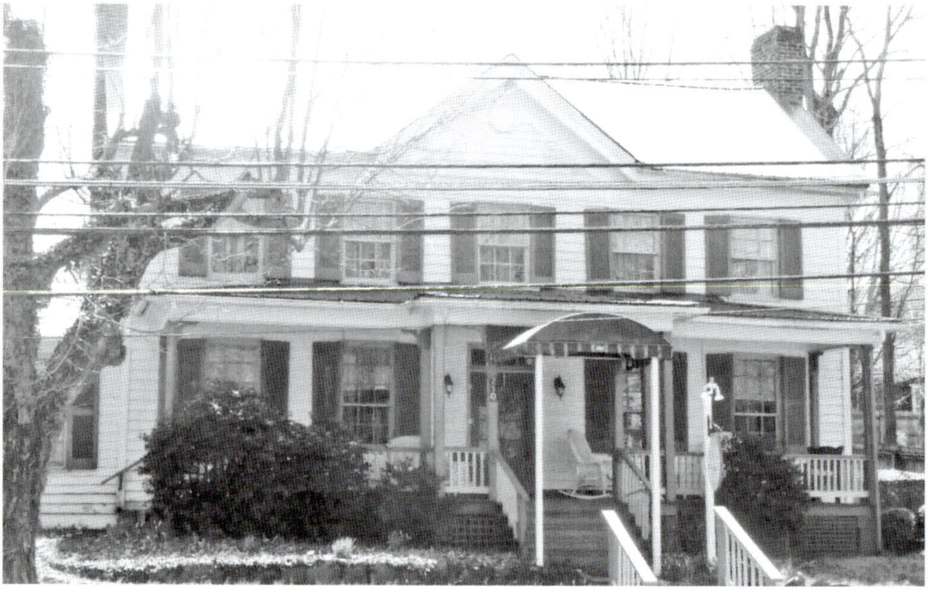

LOVE HOUSE. This two-story frame house with a central gable is located on Valley Street near Court Street. It was built in 1850 by John W. Love. Love later moved just outside Abingdon and began a school for males and females after the Civil War. After serving as a residence, the house is now operated as the popular Love House bed and breakfast. (Town of Abingdon.)

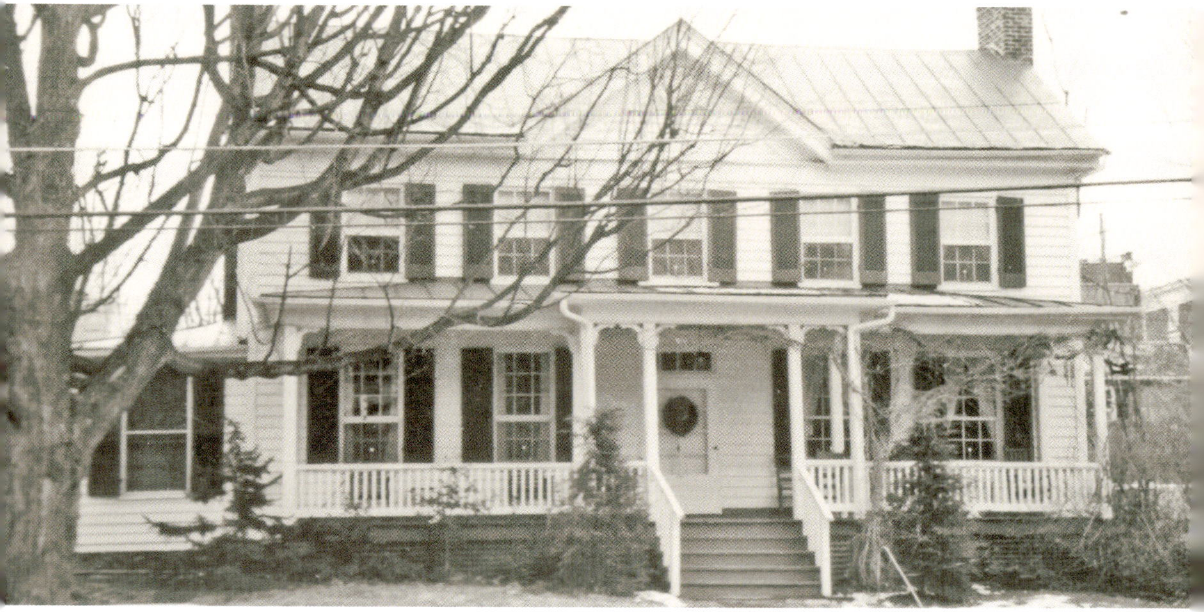

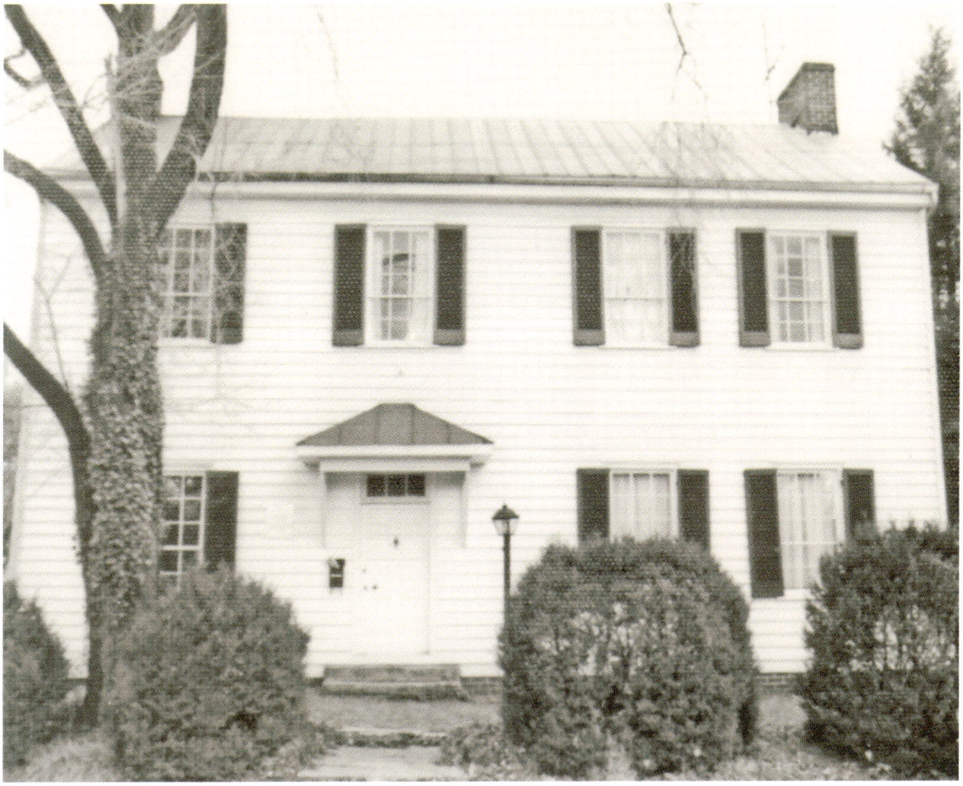

Gabriel Stickley House. This two-story frame house was built in 1836 by Gabriel Stickley, who was a local blacksmith and wagon builder. After 1854, Noble McGinnis, a clock peddler and prosperous merchant, lived in the house. The house has retained much of its architectural integrity thanks to the owners, as shown in the 1973 photograph above and the current photograph below. (Town of Abingdon.)

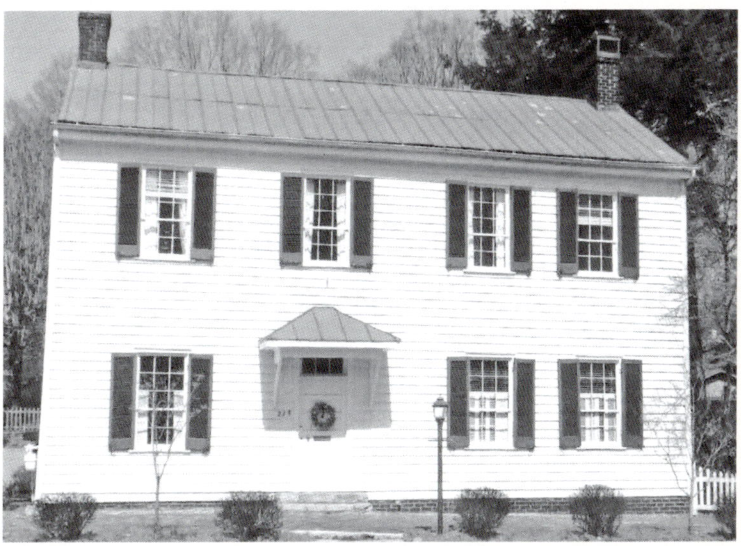

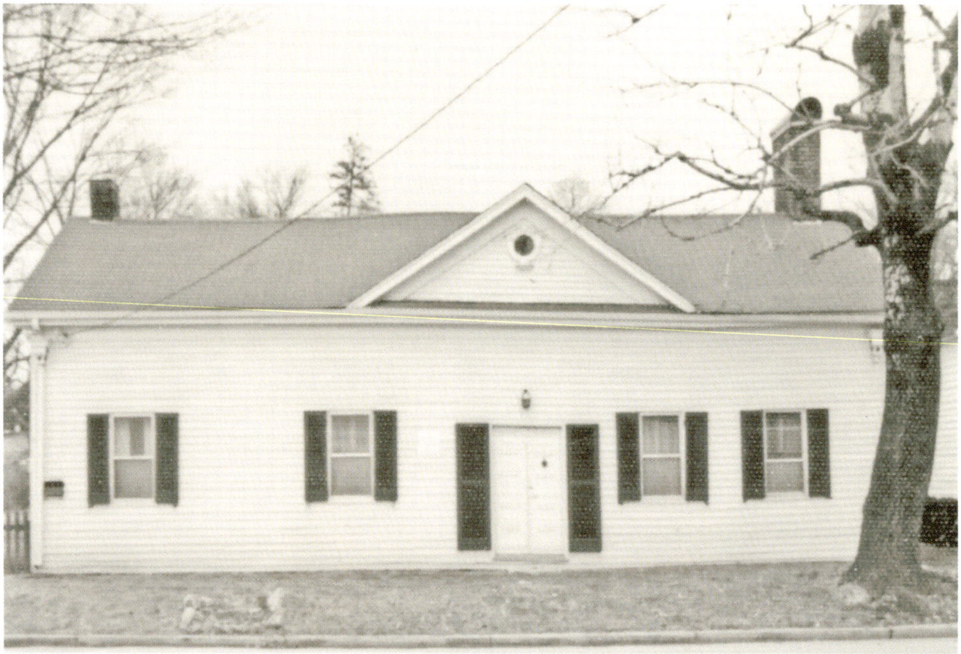

Anne Berry House. One of the earlier houses on Valley Street, the *c.* 1797 original section of this frame house may have been built by William King, a major property owner in the region who made much money from salt mines in nearby Saltville. The widow Anne Berry acquired the property in 1815. Additions and renovations have been made to the house, including finishing the loft into a second floor. Well maintained, the house provides an attractive example of early-19th-century architecture. (Town of Abingdon.)

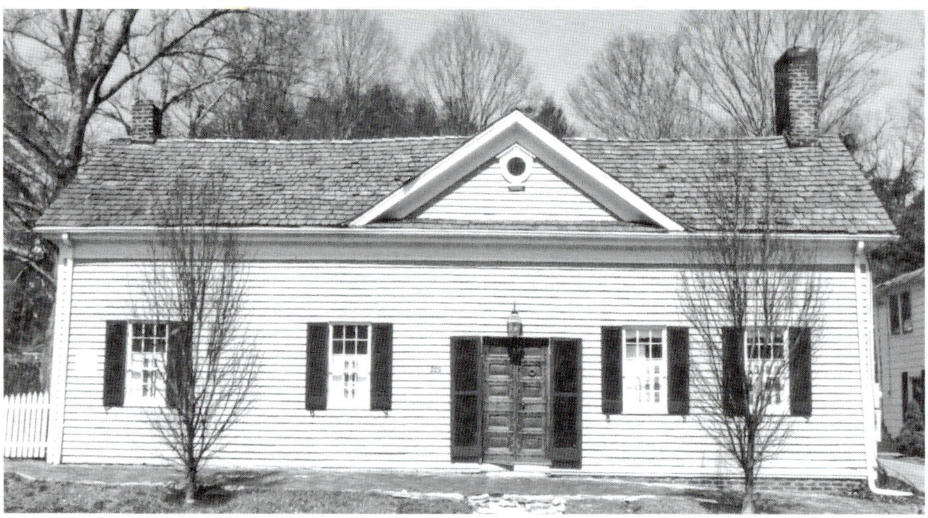

Bibliography

Davis, Edward H., and Edward B. Morgan. *The Virginia Creeper Trail Companion*. Johnson City, TN: 1997.

The Historical Society of Washington County. "Historical Houses of Washington County, Virginia," *The Historical Society of Washington County, Virginia Publications* Series II, No. 6 (Spring 1968).

King, Nanci C. *Places in Time: Volume I Abingdon, Virginia 1778–1880*. Abingdon, VA: 1989.

———. *Places in Time: Volume II Abingdon, Meadowview and Glade Spring, Virginia*. Abingdon, VA: 1994.

McGuinn, Doug. *The Virginia Creeper*. Boone, NC: Bamboo Books, 1998.

Neal, J. Allen. *Bicentennial History of Washington County, Virginia*. Dallas, TX: Taylor, 1977.

Summers, Lewis Preston. *History of Southwest Virginia 1746–1786, Washington County, 1777–1870*. Johnson City, TN: The Overmountain Press, 1989 (reprinted from the 1903 edition).

Warmuth, Donna Akers. *Abingdon, Virginia*. Charleston, SC: Arcadia Publishing, 2002.

———. *Washington County*. Charleston, SC: Arcadia Publishing, 2006.

———. *Washington County Revisited*. Charleston, SC: Arcadia Publishing, 2008.

About the Author

Donna Gayle Akers is proud to be a ninth-generation Washington County native and member of the Black's Fort Chapter of the Daughters of the American Revolution. She grew up just outside Abingdon near the Rich Valley community and White's Mill and attended Abingdon High School, James Madison University (where she received a bachelor's degree), and University of Virginia (master's degree). Combining her interests in local history, genealogy, historic preservation, and oral histories, she has compiled six books in Arcadia's Images of America series (*Abingdon*, *Washington County*, *Washington County Revisited*, *Boone*, *Blowing Rock*, and *Watauga County*), and published *Legends, Stories and Ghostly Tales of Abingdon and Washington County, Virginia* (Laurel Publishing) and a children's book, *Plumb Full of History: A Story of Abingdon, Virginia* (High Country Publishers).

Her books have received positive reviews by nationally known authors such as Lee Smith and Sharyn McCrumb, as well as the press. She has been accepted at the prestigious writing workshop at Hindman Settlement School in Kentucky, where she has studied writing with well-known authors.

Donna has received numerous regional writing awards, and published articles and stories in *Appalachian Heritage*, *Smoky Mountain Living*, *High Country News*, and *High Country Press*. She was invited to be a featured author at the Virginia Festival of the Book and has judged several writing contests.

She has written and recorded humorous anecdotes on mountain living for WNCW in Spindale, North Carolina.

She and her two sons, Owen and Riley, live near the Blue Ridge Parkway just outside Boone, North Carolina, where she researches local history, writes books, and teaches writing workshops to children and adults. Her current writing projects include a novel set in a small town strangely similar to Abingdon, as well as a Civil War era novel set at White's Mill near Abingdon.